Endorsements

Jim Steele

Having been at Salesforce to witness the birth of Customer Success, I'm excited to see a book focused on this subject around which I have so much personal passion. One of the foundations of our success at Salesforce was Customer Success so it's particularly great to see the history of the discipline, along with a glimpse at the future, documented in this book. I recommend it to every CEO or leader out there who is truly seeking to build a customer success-centric company.

—Jim Steele, President & Chief Customer Officer, Insidesales and former President & Chief Customer Officer, Salesforce (12 1/2 years)

Roger Lee

As one of the early investors in the technology of Customer Success, I'm particularly pleased to see the rapidly accelerating growth of the entire industry. The "subscription tsunami" as outlined in the book has profoundly disrupted the software world, and forced a focus on customers that did not exist previously. This book will help those who need to understand how this brave new world works, and also people looking for some practical guidance on how to execute successfully in the subscription economy. The team at Gainsight helped pioneer the Customer Success movement and definitely has the chops put together this hitchhiker's guide for those traveling the same road.

—Roger Lee, General Partner, Battery Ventures

Tien Tzuo (CEO, Zuora)

The world is moving to a Subscription Economy, and this book directly addresses that shift. Smart companies aren't trying to pitch products to strangers anymore. They're figuring out how to grow, monetize and build an ongoing, mutually beneficial relationship with a dedicated base of subscribers. Customer Success is fundamental to this process, and this book documents three core aspects—philosophy, discipline, and organization—in a sharp, practical way.

—Tien Tzuo, CEO and Founder, Zuora

Byron Deeter

At Bessemer Venture Partners, we've invested in over 100 cloud companies and have been fortunate to work with industry leaders including LinkedIn, Twilio, Pinterest, Yelp, Shopify, and Box. One recurring theme for every successful subscription-based company I've seen is a relentless focus on Customer Success. Not lip service, but true focus and passion. That's one reason I'm thrilled to finally see a book on the subject which explains not only why this is important but includes practical guidance on how to do it. I'm also really excited that it goes beyond the cloud to explore why Customer Success is critical to traditional companies and B2C companies, too. The folks at Gainsight really nailed it, and I strongly recommend this book for any executive running a high-performance organization. Understanding Customer Success leads to company success.

—Byron Deeter, Partner, Bessemer Venture Partners

Mary Trick

At Infor, the majority of our business is enterprise software so I was particularly pleased to find that this book does not align Customer Success only with cloud companies or only with edge applications, but explains why it's so critical to all software businesses. The customer economy that we're living in demands a new focus on customers no matter what kind of business you are in, and the team at Gainsight understands this well. Dan's book pulls together significant insights that will benefit all of us.

—Mary Trick, Chief Customer Officer, Infor

Mary Poppen

Customer Success is now a common business term, but this wasn't so just a few years ago. The evolution has been dramatic over the past 10 years. I've experienced this exciting evolution firsthand from what was initially a smaller SaaS company (SuccessFactors) to what it has grown to become within a large, enterprise software company (SAP). Customer Success grows in importance every day as companies recognize that the foundation of continued success and growth is built upon a satisfied and renewing customer base. While the evolution continues, the core themes that make it important have remained the same and Dan, Nick, and Lincoln captured those elements perfectly in this book. I was especially pleased to see that it went beyond a philosophical conversation about Customer Success to delve into the nitty-gritty of the practical, day-to-day driving principles every CEO and leader needs to understand.

Those of us driving the importance and evolution of Customer Success will benefit personally if all of our executives and board members understand and support it, too.
—**Mary Poppen, Chief Customer Officer, SAP SuccessFactors**

Clara Shih

Every business in the world needs to be thinking about Customer Success. No surprise it has help set companies like Salesforce apart, as I saw it play out firsthand. At Hearsay, our first hire was in Customer Success. It is the investment that keeps on giving. Congratulations to Nick and team for putting their stamp on the industry and creating this extremely valuable guide that will transform your organization.
—**Clara Shih, Founder and CEO, Hearsay Social**

CUSTOMER
SUCCESS

CUSTOMER SUCCESS

How Innovative Companies Are Reducing Churn and Growing Recurring Revenue

Nick Mehta, Dan Steinman, and Lincoln Murphy

WILEY

Published by John Wiley & Sons, Inc., Hoboken, New Jersey
Published simultaneously in Canada

For general information about our other products and services, please contact our Customer Care Department within the United States at (800) 762-2974, outside the United States at (317) 572-3993 or fax (317) 572-4002.

Wiley publishes in a variety of print and electronic formats and by print-on-demand. Some material included with standard print versions of this book may not be included in e-books or in print-on-demand. If this book refers to media such as a CD or DVD that is not included in the version you purchased, you may download this material at http://booksupport.wiley.com. For more information about Wiley products, visit www.wiley.com.

Library of Congress Cataloging-in-Publication Data:

Names: Mehta, Nick, 1977- author. | Steinman, Dan, 1958- author.
Title: Customer success : how innovative companies are reducing churn and growing recurring
    revenue / Nick Mehta, Dan Steinman.
Description: Hoboken : Wiley, 2016. | Includes index.
Identifiers: LCCN 2015040939 (print) | LCCN 2015051466 (ebook) |
    ISBN 9781119167969 (hardback : alk. paper) | ISBN 9781119168294 (pdf) |
    ISBN 9781119168300 (epub)
Subjects: LCSH: Customer relations. | Customer services. | Success in business. |
    BISAC: BUSINESS & ECONOMICS / Customer Relations.
Classification: LCC HF5415.5 .M4344 2016 (print) | LCC HF5415.5 (ebook) |
    DDC 658.8/12—dc23
LC record available at http://lccn.loc.gov/2015040939

Cover image: Tom Merton/Getty Images, Inc.
Cover design: Wiley

Printed in the United States of America

20 19 18 17 16 15 14 13 12 11

Contents

Gainsight Book Foreword

The term Customer Success has become a buzzword in today's business world. Customers all expect it, and vendors all aim to deliver it. But who decides when it's been achieved? If you are truly a customer-centric company, the answer to that—and all other questions—should come easily: The customer ultimately decides.

As this book illustrates, the cloud era has necessitated a shift to a true customer-first model, and it has also proven that customer satisfaction and customer success are not always synonymous. In a subscription model, you never stop working to win your customers. When done well, every single day is spent with a relentless focus on *their* success, not yours. Each and every customer deserves an amazing experience and an unwavering commitment to success from their vendors. But success cannot be standardized, and the companies who understand this are the ones poised to reap the greatest rewards.

Adopting a customer-first philosophy ultimately means listening to your customers and operating in ways that help them get closer to *their* customers—particularly through the embrace of cloud, mobile, social, and analytics technologies. And, of course, being truly customer-centric means having a deep understanding of your customers' unmet needs. Once you know this, you will have a great foundation on which to build the strategy, team, and mechanics that drive Customer Success in your organization.

In my role as the president of Sales and Customer Success at Salesforce, I have a unique vantage point to watch the Customer Success movement unfold. Sixteen years ago, Salesforce pioneered the concept of Customer Success. It was at the very heart of Marc Benioff's vision and, all these years and customers later, we are as committed to it as when we had just a few customers. This commitment stems from the fact that Customer Success drives everything we do. It's not just an idea or a department; it's a core value, and it's everyone's job.

In the six years since I have been at Salesforce, we have brought even more rigor to Customer Success by transforming the organization into a proactive, data-driven group that drives customer utilization, adoption, and success. My team of nearly 4,000 experts is dedicated to the mission of helping our customers get full value from our products—and ultimately transform their businesses. In my time here, I have seen firsthand the transformative power of a customer-centric culture. I have witnessed our customers soar to incredible heights by using our platform to connect with their customers in innovative ways, and I've seen our own success follow suit.

In my 30 years in technology, I have never seen the kind of mutual loyalty that exists between vendor and customer, as it does with Salesforce. I truly believe that it is because we are willing to invest in Customer Success, and customers are willing to invest in ours. That's "attitudinal loyalty," to steal a phrase from the book

Customer Success is not a one-size-fits-all proposition and it is evolving at the same accelerated pace as the technology that underpins it. Delivering success requires constantly checking in with customers and adapting products and services based on their needs. At Salesforce, we are continually reimagining our success offerings by adding expertise, innovation, and intelligence that make our customers' unique visions come to life. In fact, today we use data science technologies—including big-data analysis and sophisticated business intelligence—to accelerate time-to-value and, ultimately, success.

Like every other organization, Customer Success has to also adapt to the changing business landscape. In our case, CRM has evolved over the years from simple sales force automation into something more akin to a customer platform, covering sales, service, marketing, analytics, apps, and IoT (internet of things). As the definition and scope of CRM have grown, Salesforce has evolved from being deployed in just one instance to running a customer's entire enterprise. This has required a change in strategy for our Customer Success team as well—from a group focused primarily on the success of individual deployments to an organization with a seat at the boardroom table, assisting with business transformation.

I'm often asked how to justify the financial investment one must make in Customer Success. It is my belief that, when done right, Customer Success needs little justification at all. It preserves the company's book of business, opens up doors for additional opportunities, and creates lifelong advocates in our customers. When optimized, Customer Success is the best sales and marketing engine possible. As described in the following pages, Customer Success is more than just the right thing to do; it is a business imperative. For this reason, my team is held accountable for customer usage, adoption, and ultimately revenue. Our success is directly tied to that of our customers.

I am extremely happy to see our partners at Gainsight documenting the history of Customer Success in this book and sharing their insights into this growing discipline. This book is a wonderful guide to help companies embark on—and thrive in—their application of Customer Success to their day-to-day businesses. This is an incredible time to be a customer-centric company, and the opportunity is limitless for those who can look into the future through the lens of the customer. The future, in fact, is already here.

In Success,
Maria Martinez
President, Sales and Customer Success, Salesforce

CUSTOMER SUCCESS

Customer Success: The History, Organization, and Imperative

1

The Recurring Revenue Tsunami: Why Customer Success Is Suddenly Crucial

In the Beginning

In the spring of 2005, Marc Benioff gathered his lieutenants together for an offsite in the sleepy seaside town of Half Moon Bay, California. San Francisco–based Salesforce.com was on a roll, the likes of which has been seldom seen, even in the technology world. After a swift five-year run to a successful initial public offering (IPO) in June, the remainder of 2004 brought more good news in the form of 88 percent bookings growth. Nearly 20,000 customers had purchased the company's customer relationship management (CRM) solution, up from less than 6,000 two years prior. The year 2004 concluded with Salesforce sporting a market cap of $500 million, and that number would quadruple by the end of 2005. All charts were pointing up and to the right, just the way you'd want them if you were an employee or an investor.

The offsite was pretty typical, celebrating the success of the company, planning for continued hypergrowth as the market continued to expand, and generally mapping out a glorious future. And then David Dempsey stepped to the podium to deliver the presentation that would earn him the nickname Dr. Doom.

3

By 2005, the Irish-born Dempsey was already five years into his Salesforce career. He had spent 11 years at Oracle before moving on, just as the dotcom bubble burst. Unfazed, he and two other ex-Oracle executives approached Benioff in early 2000 with a proposal to bring Salesforce.com to the European market. After several months of negotiations, the deal was struck. Today, Dempsey is a senior vice president and the global head of renewals, which, as is the goal of all recurring revenue businesses, carries 70 to 80 percent of Salesforce's annual bookings responsibility. In 2015, that renewal number is approaching $5 billion.

When you have that kind of responsibility, you quickly begin to understand the levers of the business and what it takes to be successful. Great sales leaders and CEOs have made their careers by understanding what's happening in the market and in their businesses and by taking the necessary steps, within their control, to keep their business growing. That might require major product changes, breaking into new markets, or any number of other strategies. The same general blueprint has been followed for years. But for Dempsey, there was something distinctly different about this challenge. No one had ever done what he was trying to do. No other subscription-based business-to-business (B2B) company had ever reached the size and growth rate of Salesforce, which also meant that, before him, no one had really needed to understand the reality and nuance of subscription software renewals the way he had to.

Renewing software subscriptions is not like renewing maintenance contracts in which the hardware or software is already paid for, installed in the data center, and running critical parts of the business. And, by the way, leaving the customer a prisoner to the vendor in many ways. One of the imprisoning factors is the cost of hardware maintenance. If the hardware is critical to the company's infrastructure, then you are basically required to pay for insurance in the case of failures. Paying for maintenance is that insurance. To make things worse, the hardware vendor typically has a stranglehold on the maintenance market because they are often upgrading and replacing proprietary hardware components. Sure, over time, a few third-party options have sprung up, but vendors always keep at least 90 percent of the business, so the competition is token at best. The software maintenance business is an even better business for vendors because no one else can provide software upgrades and bug fixes for their proprietary software. So, the renewal of a maintenance contract—hardware or software—is mostly a formality, with a tiny bit of negotiation involved. Unfortunately, the assumptions about maintenance renewals carried over to the SaaS (Software as a Service) world that Dempsey and Salesforce lived in. Those assumptions were misleading at best.

The renewals Dempsey was responsible for were often battles, not givens. For most SaaS products, customers have choices. Even with 20,000 customers, Salesforce was still often as much nice-to-have as it was must-have, which is always the case in a new market, as CRM was at the time. The bottom line on SaaS renewals is that customers can, and do, choose to not renew their contracts at a much higher rate than for maintenance products. That's because they usually have choices. Other vendors in the same market offer easy conversions to their product and lower prices. Customers are not captive like they are to maintenance contracts. That's just one of many ways that the recurring revenue business model has shifted power from the vendor to the customer, and Salesforce in 2005 was no exception. Customers had choices—competitors, the option to build their own solution, or just to do without CRM altogether—and they exercised that choice. Boy, did they ever.

Into the middle of that reality strode Dempsey, understanding it in a way that no one else did because he was the man responsible for renewing Salesforce customers' contracts. The message he shared with the rest of the Salesforce executive team was not good news. The bottom line was simple and direct: despite what it looked like from the outside, Salesforce as a business was in a death spiral. Underneath the glowing results and amazing growth rates, there was a fundamental flaw in the business, and continuing on the current path would bring disaster. The culprit was summed up in one simple word—*churn*. Customers who decided they no longer wanted to be customers. Churn. A luxury afforded to customers in a recurring revenue business. Churn. A simple concept, totally part of our thinking today, but one that, in 2005, no other subscription-based B2B company had dealt with at this magnitude. Churn.

The churn rate at Salesforce was 8 percent. That doesn't sound so bad until you add these two words—*per month*! Do the math if you wish, but it will come out like this: almost every customer was exiting the business every year. Salesforce was starting to learn what every other subscription company has learned since (thank you, Salesforce). You can't pour enough business into the top of the funnel to sustain real growth if customers are leaking out the bottom at a high rate. Yes, you can show glowing growth rates for new customer acquisition, and that's a very good thing. But the allure and value of a recurring revenue business such as Salesforce is in *growing the overall value of the installed base*. That takes new customer acquisition plus high retention rates plus positive upsell results (selling more to existing customers). Only when all three of those gears are working do you have the healthy business engine that investors will reward.

Dempsey's presentation awakened Benioff and set the wheels in motion around a company-wide initiative to focus on, measure, and reduce churn. One simple, fact-based presentation delivered to the right audience at the right time started something that is only now, 10 years later, gaining full traction as a discipline and a business imperative for all recurring revenue businesses. Dr. Doom had effectively given birth to the customer success movement.

Attitudinal versus Behavioral Loyalty

Customer success is ultimately about loyalty. Every company wants loyal customers. Recurring revenue businesses, such as Salesforce, *need* loyal customers. Acquiring customers is expensive. Really expensive. That makes keeping them a necessity, no matter how big your market might be. It's simply a losing battle to try to out-acquire a high churn rate. So, if a business depends on loyalty, it's critical to understand what that word means.

Much has been written about different kinds of loyalty. The general consensus is that there are two kinds of loyalty—attitudinal loyalty and behavioral loyalty. These are sometimes referred to as emotional loyalty and intellectual loyalty. The premise is simple although the social science may be quite complex. The premise is that there are customers who are loyal because they have to be (behavioral/intellectual), and then there are customers who are loyal because they love a particular brand or product (attitudinal/emotional). As a vendor or brand, the latter is highly preferable for a variety of reasons: willingness to pay a higher price, less vulnerable to competition, more likely to advocate for "their" brand, and so forth. The housewife who shops at Hank's Grocery because it's the only place within 30 miles that sells bread and milk is behaviorally loyal. It's possible she's also attitudinally loyal (Hank could be her husband), too, but her basic loyalty is because she does not have options. That's the extreme example, but we're probably all behaviorally loyal to a variety of products. I get gas at the same place 90 percent of the time because it's convenient and, based on very little research, a good price. The fact that they shut down their credit card machines for 10 minutes at 7:00 every morning is annoying because that's exactly when I'm on my way to work. They don't know it, except for the cashier I expressed my frustration to one day, but this creates the opposite of attitudinal loyalty for me. Fortunately for them, the convenience continues to win the day for now. But they are vulnerable to another station popping up nearby, priced similarly, and with credit card shutdowns at 3 A.M. instead of 7 A.M. or, better yet, who has figured out that it's important not to shut down the credit card machines at all.

Attitudinal loyalty is much harder to create and sustain because it's expensive. It's expensive to build products that customers love instead of products that they simply own. It's expensive to create an experience that delights instead of one that just tries to not annoy. When my daughter was graduating from high school, she needed a laptop computer. What was it that caused her to stomp her foot and insist on a Mac when the Dell options were functionally comparable and much less expensive? The logical conversation I attempted with her did not move her an inch. Despite the fact that she couldn't cite a single speed, function, or quality argument for the Mac, her heart was set and her mind made up. I still don't know why (but she did get her Mac). Maybe it was because the cool kids all had one. Maybe it was because she loved her iPod. Maybe it was because she just liked jeans and black turtlenecks. I honestly don't know. But now I know what to call it—attitudinal loyalty or, in her case, more appropriately, emotional loyalty (because the discussion did include tears). And that's the kind of loyalty we all long for in our customers.

Apple has been chronicled in so many ways—papers, books, movies—that I will do it no justice here in comparison. It did something with regard to loyalty that looks and feels like magic but clearly isn't. There's just a certain quality to Apple's product, packaging, advertising, and presentation, and it creates not only a purchase but also an experience that somehow touches an emotional chord. Steve Jobs figured out how to create attitudinal loyalty perhaps better than anyone, before or since. And it's literally priceless. The fanaticism of Apple's loyal customers carried it through a very dark time when products weren't very good and its business teetered on the edge.

Apple came out on the other side with virtually all of its loyal fans (some weren't even customers) intact, and, then, when it started to make products that partially justified that fanaticism, the ride to the top (most valuable company in history) was full-speed ahead.

So, what's the point, and how does it relate to customer success? Customer Success is designed to create attitudinal loyalty. Marc Benioff and Salesforce figured it out and, over the past 10 years, have invested massive amounts of time and money into customer success. Behavioral loyalty wasn't really an option in the early years because Salesforce was never going to be the only game in town, and customers weren't sticky because they hadn't invested emotionally or financially into the integrations and processes that make switching really expensive. One could argue that lots of Salesforce customers today are behaviorally loyal because the product has become central to the way they do business and too difficult to swap out. But many of those customers are also attitudinally loyal—check out Dreamforce (their annual conference) sometime if you don't believe it—and that's the best of both worlds.

Steve Jobs also knew that attitudinal loyalty was critical, and, in addition to creating it with elegant and beautiful products, he also invested in customer success. But, being the marketing guru that he was, he came up with a different name for it—Genius Bar. When Apple decided to create retail stores, the naysayers were loud and numerous. Hadn't history proved that retail stores for computers didn't work (RIP Gateway)? What Jobs banked on correctly was that retail stores for a consumer technology brand, at least one with a core fanatical following, could work. And, of course, it did. One could argue that the publicity derived from the long lines outside Apple stores three days before the release of the new iPhone was worth the investment in all the stores combined. But Jobs took it one step further. He didn't settle for having stores only showing off and selling his products, no matter how many helpful salespeople there were in every store. He also created a place in the back of the store staffed with customer success managers. We'll explore in detail what we mean by *customer success manager* later in this book, but the simple role definition is this: individuals that help customers get the most value out of your products. That's clearly what Apple Store geniuses are intended to do. It wasn't cheap for Apple to decide to have 10 or 20 geniuses on the payroll at every single store. As we said, attitudinal loyalty is not cheap. But it changed the nature of the relationship between vendor and customer by personalizing it and extending it beyond the purchase. That's something that very few business-to-consumer (B2C) or retail companies have figured out how to do. Maybe Zappos and Nordstrom have with their emphasis on customer service. Maybe Amazon has in a different way by adding Prime to its offerings. But I bet you can't think of a lot more. Interestingly, we all know that some of the geniuses at the Apple Store are not really geniuses at all. Many of us have even had frustrating experiences with them. The fact that they exist to touch and help real customers and build even the slightest relationship drives attitudinal loyalty. That's the art of customer success. Most vendors don't start with the fanaticism and loyalty that Apple does (a two-edged sword by the way), but we desperately want our customers to become advocates, not just customers. We need attitudinal loyalty not just behavioral loyalty. Customer success is the means to that end.

Marc Benioff created customer success out of his need to reduce churn. Steve Jobs created customer success out of his intuition that it would increase attitudinal loyalty to Apple products. We're lucky today that we can follow in the footsteps of two icons who have proved that customer success works regardless of your business model. It may seem more obvious, and more imperative, in a recurring revenue business, but it can be no less valuable in a traditional consumer business.

Tien Tzuo was the eleventh employee at Salesforce and, not coincidentally, in the room in Half Moon Bay for Dr. Doom's presentation. He is currently the CEO at Zuora, where he coined the phrase *the subscription economy* to describe the changing landscape as traditional businesses were getting disrupted by the move to a recurring revenue model. He also said, although he may not have been the first, "In traditional businesses, the customer relationship ends with the purchase. But in a subscription business, the customer relationship begins with the purchase." That's a powerful distinction and Benioff and Jobs both realized it and invested heavily in it. Benioff created the most successful subscription-based software company in history. And Jobs brought the subscription thinking and attitude into a nonsubscription business in a way not previously done. Many other traditional companies will choose the same path in the coming years, while recurring revenue businesses will not have the luxury of choice.

The Subscription Tsunami

Customer success sounds like a catchy phrase your marketing team might come up with, doesn't it? Or a mantra some PR firm concocted for their CEO to make it sound like she really does care about customers. But in today's recurring revenue businesses, customer success is much more than a catchy phrase or a slick marketing campaign. It's a necessary part of any subscription business, as Mr. Benioff and Salesforce proved, and it requires investment, attention, and leadership. It's not lip service around "putting customers first" or "the customer is king." Those phrases sound good but such campaigns often start off with a bang and then fizzle quickly unless they are driven by a passionate and charismatic leader (like Tony Hsieh) or by a business imperative. Customer success, as we'll discuss throughout this book, falls squarely into the latter category. It does not require a passionate or charismatic leader, although that helps, because it's nothing less than life or death in the subscription economy.

Real organizational change in business is rare. Think about our organizations today—sales, marketing, product development, finance, and services. Those have been the fundamental components of an enterprise for hundreds of years despite the enormity of change within the business world during that time. One could argue that human resources is new, but the reality is that it was always being done, just not led by a separate organization. As far as fundamental organizations go, information technology (IT) might be the only truly new invention in the past 70 years, driven obviously by the ubiquity of technology in every aspect of our jobs. Customer success is the next big organization change. As with IT, customer success is becoming a thing because something else is changing—in this case, the business model. Subscriptions are all the rage. From software to music to movies to diet programs. The way to the heart of investors and the public markets is to establish a business that creates monthly recurring payments from lots and lots of customers. If Wall Street and the investment community love something, so do the CEOs. If a business is not subscriptionable, it is probably becoming pay-as-you-go, which has all the same characteristics and imperatives. Subscriptions are obviously not new, but the movement of existing businesses from a nonsubscription business model to a subscription model most certainly is. Everyone is searching for a recurring revenue component to their business model and, ideally, the whole business, not just a component. This 15-year-old movement started with the software world, but the splash caused by that boulder is rippling across virtually every other industry, too.

Thus, the need for this book. The subscription tsunami is well under way and having a massive impact on the software world. Customer success is one of the secondary waves being drawn in behind the tsunami. But customer success is not only a new organization but also a philosophy sweeping its way into nonsoftware, nontechnology, and non-B2B companies. It may not have been referred to as *customer success* until recently, but it's happening everywhere, as witnessed by the Apple story, driven by technology and the availability of information (i.e., the Internet). No matter what kind of business you are in, now is the time to understand what to do about this wave. Let's start by exploring the origins of customer success in B2B software because that's where this all began.

Software is eating the world. That statement was only slightly controversial when Marc Andreesen first wrote his famous essay in 2011.

"Why Software Is Eating The World"—http://www.wsj.com/articles/SB10001424053111903480904576512250915629460

Today, his notion has moved from bold and futuristic to indisputable. If there's any truth to it at all, it's critical that every business leader understands what is happening in Silicon Valley. The software industry has gone through a dramatic transition over the past 15 years, and the customer is at the center of this transition. This change has been driven by the ubiquity of the Internet and the advent of that thing called *the cloud*. In fact, the farther away we are from the beginning of this transition, the clearer the bifurcation between the way things were done BC (before cloud) and AC (after cloud). The change has altered almost every aspect of the way a software company works but is best understood through the lens of the customer. In particular, B2B software customers AC differ from BC customers in two very important ways:

1. How they purchase software
2. How their lifetime value (LTV) is realized

These two themes are closely related. In fact, number 1 is the reason for number 2. To be truly precise, the major difference in the purchasing process is not really *how* customers purchase a software product but *that* they purchase a software product. In the days BC, unlike today, the purchase transaction actually did result in a change of ownership. This model, commonly referred to as a *perpetual license*, passed ownership rights to use the software from the vendor to the customer at the time of the transaction. Because of the singular nature of this transaction, the vendor needed to maximize the monetary value of it in order for its business model to work. The result was that the cost of the initial software purchase was relatively very high, not to mention the associated hardware costs. For a software company, especially enterprise B2B, this was the only path to profitability (yes, there was a time when that mattered).

A consumer scenario, which might bring back memories for some of you, helps to illustrate how dramatic this change has been. When I was 16 years old, I fell in love with a song I heard on the radio, "Bohemian Rhapsody" by Queen. It was amazing and complex and needed to be listened to over and over (although my mother might disagree with that last point). The only way to accomplish that goal in those days was to purchase the album ("A Night at the Opera," for those who care). So that's what I did. I went to my nearest music store and plunked down $16.99 for the 8-track (if you don't know, look it up), a lot of money for a 16-year-old kid at that time. Basically, I paid $17 for one song. To play and listen to that song, I also had to have a pretty expensive stereo system. You know, the ones with the three-foot-tall speakers that doubled as bar stools. And that's the way it was—$1,000 stereo system and $17 for the album to listen to one song. This was basically the consumer music ownership experience for the better part of 50 years. The first major change, other than format and not counting Napster, in how we consumed music came thanks to Apple—the ability to purchase just one song for 99 cents on iTunes. This was revolutionary (it literally started a revolution) for the music industry. In fact, it fundamentally changed it forever, but the analogy to the software world was only completed when streaming music services, such as Pandora and Spotify, came along. No longer are songs even purchased. They are leased, and, depending on how much music you listen to, the cost per song may be down to pennies or even less. I could have listened to "Bohemian Rhapsody" thousands of times through my computer (purchased primarily for other reasons) for only a few bucks. Thankfully, for all us parents, this change was accompanied by the invention of earbuds and small and inexpensive personal music players (PMP). What drove this change in how we purchase (or lease) music? Technology and the Internet. The very same drivers that changed the way companies purchase their CRM system. (See Table 1.1.)

Music

Table 1.1 Consuming Music Before and After the Cloud

	Before Cloud	**After Cloud**
Ownership	Album	None—lease/subscription
Price	$1/song	$.01/song
Quantity	15 songs	Millions of songs
Hardware	Stereo	PMP/phone/computer
	Big speakers	Earbuds
Hardware price	$1,000+	$50 PMP, $0 for existing devices
Availability	Home/car	Anywhere

Software—Siebel versus Salesforce

In those days BC, it was common for a software deal, such as the Siebel one approximated in Table 1.2, to be a multimillion-dollar transaction. It was also common for that initial deal to constitute more than 50 percent of all the money the vendor would collect from that customer over its lifetime. In the earliest days, before software maintenance fees, that percentage might even exceed 80 or 90 percent. Contrast that with the Salesforce example (AC), and you'll begin to understand point 2—the realization of LTV from each customer over a much longer period.

It's not hard to grasp what happened and why. Let's say I'm the CEO of a software company, and I sell you my solution for $3 million. I'm well aware at that point that all of the additional money I will collect from you over your lifetime as my customer is maybe another $500,000. Given that reality, your value to me diminishes dramatically the moment your $3 million is in my bank account. That's not to say that I, or any past or current CEOs, don't care about customers. Of course we do. As we all know, customers have value beyond what they pay us—references, case studies, word-of-mouth,

Table 1.2   Consuming Software Before and After the Cloud

	Before Cloud	After Cloud
Ownership	Application	None—lease/subscription
Price	$2 million	$2,000–$20,000/month
Hardware	Servers	Included in subscription
	Networking	Included in subscription
	Storage	Included in subscription
Hardware price	$2 million	Included in subscription
Time to install	9–24 months	0–6 months
People	Lots	Few
Availability	Office	Anywhere

and so on. But that additional value, even if you include the future monetary value that comes from the purchase of more products, licenses, and maintenance fees, does not change the fundamental viability of my business. I can still survive, even thrive, based exclusively on my ability to continue to sell new customers for that same price. I may care passionately about my customer's success, but if it doesn't matter to the bottom line whether they get value or even use my solution, then I'm highly unlikely to invest significantly in ensuring their success. It was this reality that led to the birth of the term *shelfware*. That was just a cheeky way to describe software that wasn't being used by the customer. That still happens today by the way. SaaS did not solve the adoption problem by any means. It just matters a lot more now than it did back then.

Although lots of B2B software is still purchased the old way, the tide has forever shifted. Today, the vast majority of software companies are using this new model in which the software is never actually purchased but leased. With this new model, SaaS, customers do not own your software; they pay for the use of it on a subscription basis with a time-limited commitment. Many software companies lease their software on a month-to-month basis while others require an annual contract or longer. But, in all cases, there's an end date to the subscription, which requires a renewal. This, then, is the subscription economy. No more paying a large, onetime fee up-front; instead, software is leased on a short-term commitment. Another related wave takes the subscription concept one step further into a pay-as-you-go model. Google AdWords and Amazon Web Services are examples of pay-as-you-go. In both models, customers have become significantly more important because their LTV really matters, not only what they pay in the initial transaction. Therein lies the need for a philosophy and an organization—customer success.

Simply put, customer success is the organization or philosophy designed to drive success for the customer. That sounds amazingly obvious, but, as we mentioned earlier, there was a time when the success of our customers was not really a business imperative. That's no longer true. You see, successful recurring revenue customers today do two very important things:

1. They remain your customers.
2. They buy more stuff from you.

It's a fundamental reality for CEOs today that, if their customers aren't taking both of those actions, their business has no chance of success. The economics just don't work. And that is why customer success has become an imperative. We'll circle back here after we take a brief look at the origins of the subscription economy, which really started with the development of SaaS. Understanding the history is important because all recurring revenue businesses are following in the footsteps of the earliest SaaS companies.

The Birth of Software as a Service

In the fall of 1995, John McCaskey walked into the Stanford Bookstore in Palo Alto, California, and bought several books, *Foundations of World Wide Web Programming with HTML & CGI*, *HTML & CGI Unleashed*, and O'Reilly's *Programming Perl* among them. At the time, McCaskey was a marketing director working for a company named Silicon Graphics (SGI). Despite his marketing title, McCaskey was an engineer at heart, and his new book collection had a purpose greater than simply a hobby. His intent was to reprogram an internal application, lightly used by the SGI marketing community, called MYOB (mine your own business). MYOB was a business intelligence (BI) tool, built on top of Business Objects. Its intent was to provide insights to the marketers regarding the sales of their products. As McCaskey's version started to take shape, it became known as MYOB Lite.

That very same year, on the other side of town, Paul Graham, self-proclaimed hacker and future Silicon Valley icon, and his friends Robert Morris and Trevor Blackwell were starting a company called Viaweb. Viaweb was also the name of their application, originally known as Webgen, which allowed users to build and host their own online stores with little technical expertise.

Both MYOB Lite and Viaweb were wildly successful. MYOB Lite caught fire at SGI because of its ease of access and use and was quickly adopted and used by 500-plus marketers and executives. Viaweb, on the other hand, was a commercial success. By the end of 1996, more than 70 stores were online, and by the end of 1997, that number had grown to more than 500. In July 1998, Graham and company sold Viaweb for $50 million in Yahoo! stock, and it became known as Yahoo Stores. He went on to form Y Combinator, a wildly successful technology incubator, out of which has come many great companies including Dropbox and Airbnb.

In addition to their real-world success and the springboard they provided for their inventors, Viaweb and MYOB Lite had one other very important thing in common. The user interface (UI) consisted only of an off-the-shelf Web browser. Paul Graham referred to Viaweb as an *application service provider*, and John McCaskey's application was simply a light version of a Business Objects implementation, sans Business Objects. In other words, Viaweb and MYOB Lite were two of history's first SaaS applications. *SaaS* is today's term for applications that do not require any client-side software. The only product needed to run them on the user side is a web browser. Today, there are thousands of SaaS applications. We use them every day—Facebook, Dropbox, Amazon, eBay, Match.com, Salesforce.com, and virtually every other software application developed in the past five years. But, in 1995, the concept was revolutionary and initiated a seismic shift in the software industry.

SaaS truly changed everything. Buyers of software not only could now lease it instead of purchase it, but do so for a much smaller financial commitment (see Table 1.2). In addition, they no longer needed to purchase expensive hardware on which to run that software and costly data centers in which to put that hardware. Remember that expensive stereo system we discussed earlier? That was the music equivalent of the BC software world's data center. They also didn't need to hire and pay for expensive employees to run those data centers and manage the new software. Applications still ran on servers, but those servers were now owned and maintained by the vendor, not the customer, and were accessed and operated through a web browser and a URL. Today, most of those data centers have been consolidated by a few companies who provide hosting and security and easy extension of the infrastructure as needed so the software vendors often don't even host their own software any longer. This critical task is usually outsourced to companies such as Amazon Web Services and Rackspace.

SaaS → Subscriptions → Customer Success

This shift to SaaS as the new way of delivering software led directly to the most important change of all—subscription-based licensing. It kind of made sense that if customers no longer had to purchase hardware to run applications, they shouldn't have to purchase the software either. In the past, the cost of hardware, data centers, security, and the people required to run everything were absorbed by the customer. But today, all of those elements of a solution are provided by the vendor, along with the software, and that has paved the way for subscriptions as the vendor's pricing model. Before the Cloud, software had also always been purchased and owned by the customer—the "perpetual license" we mentioned earlier. But the rise of the Internet and SaaS as a delivery model created the option, for many now the only option, to simply lease the software. We often refer to these subscriptions today as "software subscriptions" but in reality, the customer is really leasing not only the software, but also some portion of the entire infrastructure required to run it, typically on monthly or annual contracts.

These two changes happened almost simultaneously and are inextricably linked, but they are worth distinguishing here. SaaS is simply the delivery model that allows applications to be run through a web browser as opposed to being shipped on CDs or digitally to customers to run on their own computers. And subscriptions are merely the payment method. These two concepts are so tightly related that a reference to SaaS today almost always refers to both the delivery and payment method.

It's hard to overstate the magnitude of this earthquake and the impact it has had on the software industry and the ripples it's creating beyond software. SaaS (referring to both components) has changed the way everyone thinks about software, from Wall Street to Main Street. Take finance, for example. SaaS requires the need to reconsider almost everything about the way company financials are kept and reported. Revenue is no longer king but has been replaced by annual recurring revenue (ARR). Profitability in the SaaS world is no longer feasible to expect in the first few years of a company's life because the up-front costs incurred to acquire and implement a new customer are so large while the monthly payments are comparatively small. But Wall Street has recognized the long-term value of a growing installed base that keeps paying for the software month after month and year after year. Check out the market caps for public SaaS companies such as Salesforce, HubSpot, and Box and compare them to the metric that used to be the stock investors' primary indicator of a company's worth—earnings per share (EPS). EPS for the companies just mentioned are mostly nonexistent because there are no earnings. And yet those companies are valued anywhere from $2 billion to $50 billion. Why is that? It's because they all have a growing set of existing customers who never stop paying for the software and who get more profitable every year they remain a customer. Wait a minute. Remember the Salesforce story with which we started the book? There's no guarantee that it's a growing set of customers who never stop paying. That's where customer success comes in.

Perhaps the most important effect of all of this—SaaS as a delivery method and subscriptions as a payment method—is that much of the power in the B2B transaction has shifted from the vendor to the customer. Think about it. The customer no longer has to buy the hardware or the software, set up and run data centers, or hire expensive people to manage all of it. They simply lease the whole package from the vendor. That also means that they can stop using it and paying for it almost any time they want. For the customer, this dramatically reduces both the up-front costs and the risk of acquiring a new solution as those costs and risks shift over to the vendor. True, there are still typically some switching costs in changing SaaS solutions but nothing like what it was in the past with perpetual-license software. At the extreme, to use a B2C analogy, it's like switching from Amazon.com to BarnesandNoble.com (both SaaS solutions) to buy a book. If you are an Amazon customer, you have probably given it your credit card info, all the addresses where you ship books, plus you've learned how to navigate the website (product) to find and purchase what you want even to the point of one-click buying and "free" shipping through Prime. That means there's some pain in deciding to purchase your next book on BarnesandNoble.com instead. You'll have to figure out how to find the book you want, put it in your shopping cart, and then go through the checkout process, providing your credit card information and shipping address. It may not be terribly painful, but it's not quite free either. The complexity and costs of switching B2B software solutions are much higher than the consumer example, but, as we've said before, it's far more doable (and likely) today than it was in the old enterprise software world. This risk is now owned almost exclusively by the software vendor.

The rise of the Internet, with easy access to virtually all the information in the world, is the culprit here. Let's examine the process of buying a new car as another illustration from the consumer world. It used to be that most of the car-buying process was controlled by the car company and specifically by the salesperson. We learned most of what we came to know about the car from him. We understood the features and options and which ones came with which package by talking to him. We negotiated the final price *only* by talking to him (and his boss). In short, control of the entire process was very much in the hands of the salesperson. Now fast-forward to 2015. Our research on the car we want is done on the Internet. We can literally get the entire bill of materials for the car if we wish. We can find out the prices from a variety of dealers, how much the value of the car will depreciate in the first year or two, how much the dealer will get in kickbacks from the manufacturer, as well as something your salesperson could not possibly know—how well that car is liked by 10 of our Facebook friends. By the time we decide to walk onto the lot for a test drive, we know more than the salesperson does about that car. The Internet has shifted the power from the dealership and the salesperson into our hands. Revolutionary.

The process of purchasing B2B software has been irrevocably altered in much the same way. The up-front costs are lower, the resource requirements are reduced, the commitment level is diminished, and the switching costs are far less than in the past. Plus, there is no shortage of access to others who have purchased and used the solution, many of whom you may know directly. Once again, the power has shifted in a dramatic way from the seller to the buyer.

And isn't this the way the world should work? Shouldn't the buyer be more in control than the seller? Shouldn't a solution have to work for the customer in order for them to continue to pay for it? Shouldn't it be relatively easy to switch to what you think is a better solution if you choose to? Shouldn't the vendor have to earn your business every month and every year? Of course, of course, of course. This is the way the retail world has always worked. If you don't like your experience at Macy's or you don't think you got value for your money, you don't have to go back. You aren't locked in to buying all your clothes from Macy's because you signed a contract three years ago and paid them $32,000. You can just walk over to Kohl's and give them a try. Your Macy's credit card won't work over there, but that's a minor inconvenience for a better solution or an improved experience.

Let's take a pause for a quick SaaS financial tutorial because it's relevant to everything else in this book. We made mention earlier to ARR as the primary measurement of a SaaS company's business. ARR stands for annual recurring revenue. It's also often referred to as ACV, or annual contract value. By either acronym, it is simply the annualized amount that customers are paying on a recurring basis for the software. If a company has 20 customers all paying $1,000 per month, the company's ARR is 20 × $1000 × 12 or $240,000. If a company has six customers all on two-year contracts worth $2 million each, that company's ARR is 6 × $2 million/2 or $6 million. Total company ARR, or ACV, is an assessment of the annualized value of the installed base. Many companies look at these same numbers monthly instead of annually and that's referred to as MRR.

Without trying to provide you with an MBA in SaaS finance, there's one more thing that has to be understood here because it leads us to the reason for this book and that is the changing value of that existing set of customers. In a perfectly predictable world using our previous examples, the 20 or 6 customers of our theoretical companies continue to be customers and pay their $12,000 or $1 million per year. Now that's perfectly predictable but not perfect by any means. In a perfect world, those customers actually pay you more money every year either because prices go up, discounts go down, they buy more licenses, or they buy additional products from you. That's how a company with $6 million in ARR could become a company with $8 million of ARR *without ever selling their software to another new customer*. This is an important and fundamental element of a successful subscription-based company—growing the value of the installed base.

Unfortunately, as with most things in life, there's an opposing edge to that sword. The value of your installed base can also shrink. Customers decide they no longer want to be customers (the Salesforce story). Customers negotiate deeper discounts when they renew their contracts. Customers may stay customers but give you back a product or licenses. All of these actions reduce your ARR as a company. As a whole, this is called *churn*. Churn is simply a measure of dollars that used to be part of your ARR that no longer are. Churn is also often used to refer to a customer that is no longer a customer. That becomes a *customer who churned*. In the broader sense of the reduction in ARR, these are referred to as churned dollars.

So at last we are approaching the heart of the matter—the management of your installed base. Growing your recurring revenue and reducing churn. You see, there is no world where these things happen without some kind of intervention or, at the very least, nurturing. Customers and vendors tend to drift apart if neither party takes any action. They are like two boats side-by-side in the middle of a lake but with no one in either boat. Inevitably, those two boats will not remain side-by-side, and probably not even in proximity. Someone has to be in at least one of the boats, preferably both, and with oars to keep them next to each other. In our SaaS world, and every recurring revenue business, this is no longer just a nice idea. It's an imperative.

Perhaps the most significant advantage of SaaS for the vendor is that it tends to expand the market for your products. With both the up-front cost and the time-to-value dramatically reduced, more and more companies become part of the target market. And few things increase a company's value more than an expanding addressable market. Using Salesforce as an example again, we've already touched on the cost component. But what about the time-to-value equation? An implementation of Siebel in 2002 might very well have taken 18 months or more. Construction of the data center, installation of the hardware, and then the complex installation, configuration, and customization of the application were part of the landscape for every customer. Some would have felt very lucky to be completed in 18 months. With Salesforce, you can literally go to their website, provide a credit card, get a login, and be putting accounts, contacts, and opportunities into the system in less than an hour. A functioning CRM system in 60 minutes?

Figure 1.1   No Software Logo

Unimaginable before SaaS. Salesforce took the idea to the extreme, even incorporating the concept of "no software" into their logo (see Figure 1.1).

There were other companies early to the SaaS party, NetSuite among them, who were also standing on Paul Graham's shoulders and making this new model enterprise-viable. Despite other SaaS companies popping up around the same time, Salesforce's success and style got people's attention, and its IPO in 2004 left little doubt that the software business model had changed forever. And for good reason. Investors were not rewarding Salesforce because the idea of SaaS was unique. They were rewarding Salesforce because the model worked. But for it to *really* work, as we've already discussed, churn has to be controlled, and the vehicle for controlling churn is called customer success. And when SaaS's most successful company built a customer success team and started talking about it publicly, it gave permission to all other subscription-based businesses to do the same. And the customer success movement began.

As we mentioned earlier, in the days prior to SaaS and subscriptions, B2B software was sold on a perpetual license basis and that meant big up-front payments. With SaaS, the equation is turned upside-down. It is not uncommon for the initial financial commitment by a customer to a SaaS company to be less than 10 percent of the expected LTV of that customer. In the case of a monthly subscription business, that number may well be less than 1 percent. Let's look at a vendor who offers its software on annual contracts, and let's say a customer pays for the first year up front to the tune of $25,000. Now, assume the customer remains a customer for eight years. That means they'll have to renew that one-year contract seven times and, if you build in an annual growth rate of 7 percent for the increase in price and additional licenses and products likely to be purchased, you'll see that the LTV of that customer will exceed 10 times the initial outlay. This, then, is the definition of the term we've been throwing around, LTV. LTV is the total dollars a customer spends (or is expected to spend) with a vendor during their relationship and is another key metric for a SaaS company.

For most software companies, the cost of acquiring a new customer is very high. All of the marketing expenses required to generate leads and then the cost of expensive sales teams to convert those leads into real customers adds up. In addition, the costs associated with getting customers up and running with a fully configured solution can be heavy and are obviously front-end weighted. In most cases, it takes 24 months or more of subscription revenue just to recover the cost of acquisition and onboarding. If customers are on annual subscriptions, as is often the case, they need to renew their contract with a vendor at least twice in order for the vendor to break even and start making a profit. Churn greatly exacerbates this challenge. And the urgency is even higher because most churn happens in the first couple of years because of the complexity of onboarding and adoption. CEOs of SaaS companies have learned very quickly that customers really are king and that real investment is required to make them successful and to retain them for long periods of time. That's the financial imperative for all recurring revenue businesses and the impetus for customer success.

Customer success is really three different, but closely related, concepts:

1. An organization
2. A discipline
3. A philosophy

At its essence, customer success is the organization that focuses on the customer experience with the goal of maximizing retention and LTV. Only if this is done effectively can a subscription company survive, and market domination comes only to those who do it exceedingly well.

Customer success has also become a new discipline. Like any other discipline—sales or product management or customer support—there are groups and forums and best practices and conferences created to support and nurture this new craft and its practitioners, into a place alongside the other necessary roles in a successful company. Individuals practicing the discipline of customer success are often called customer success managers (CSMs) but can be found with a variety of titles, including account managers, customer relationship managers, customer advocates, and client specialists, among many others. In this book, we'll often refer to CSM as the generic term covered by all of those titles.

And last, customer success is a philosophy, and it must pervade the entire company. No organization, or job role, can function in a vacuum, and customer success may be the best example of this. It requires a top-down, company-wide commitment to truly deliver world-class customer success.

It is these three principles that are the focus of the remainder of this book.

2 | The Customer Success Strategy: The New Organization versus the Traditional Business Model

Why Does Customer Success Matter?

Before we dig into the organizational aspects of customer success, let's talk about the desired outcomes that drive the accompanying investment. This is important because the way you organize for customer success will often be driven by your primary motivations for investing in it. There are three basic benefits that come from executing customer success well:

1. Reduce/manage churn.
2. Drive increased contract value for existing customers.
3. Improve the customer experience and customer satisfaction.

Reduce/manage churn. As we explored in Chapter 1, using the early days of Salesforce as an example, churn can be the killer of a recurring revenue business. If churn is too high, one solution is to invest in customer success. It's important to understand that investing in customer success cannot make up for fundamental flaws in other parts of the enterprise. If your product is not good enough or your implementation processes do not meet customer requirements or your sales team is continually setting improper expectations, you will fail regardless of the quality of your customer success efforts. All things being competitively equal, an investment in the people, processes, and technology for delivering customer success will result in a reduction in churn if it's too high or a management of churn if it's at or near an acceptable and sustainable level. The specific financial benefits will depend on the size of your installed base.

The negative impact of churn goes beyond financial results, too. Companies always consist of people, so when companies churn, people are affected. Those people know other people, and negative publicity can spread quickly. If your product touched, or was used by, lots of people, the negative impact can be viral. There's also a very good chance that a customer who churns from you buys from your competitor. This means you get dinged twice. It's like losing a game in a pennant race to the team you are chasing—you lose one and they win one. It's a double-whammy and very painful in a competitive market, exacerbated further when that ex-customer becomes a reference for your competitor (which they will do anything and everything to make happen). These are negative second-order effects. We'll talk about positive second-order effects in a minute.

Drive increased contract value for existing customers. This is usually referred to as *upsell and cross-sell*, but those terms don't always mean the same thing to everyone, so I avoid them when I can. Simply, it means selling more stuff (recurring revenue stuff) to your existing customers. Some companies don't have a churn problem because their products are inherently sticky or because the expense and effort of implementing them is significantly large. Workday would be an example of the latter situation. Very few of its customers have ever churned. But that doesn't mean customer success is unnecessary or unimportant. Workday invests significantly in customer success to ensure against the possibility of churn, but, more specifically, to deliver additional bookings/revenue to the company bottom line from the installed base. Consider a company whose average customer increases its spend or contract value by 30 percent annually. That's an extremely positive metric, but it leads to an interesting view of the customer who expands by only 10 percent. There's no churn. In fact, the net retention number for that customer is 110 percent. Many companies would kill for that average.

However, for this company and that customer, significant revenue is being left on the table as compared with the average. Because it's been proved that average customers (not just great ones) are growing at 30 percent, it's reasonable to assume that applying customer success to those below-average customers will bring them up closer to the average. In situations like this, you basically want to treat that 20 percent deficit as if it is churn and aggressively seek to remedy it. If your existing base of customers is sufficiently large, moving the overall net retention from 130 to 137 percent will have a significant bottom line impact. Pushing those 110 percent customers closer to 130 percent will have that exact impact and might easily justify an increased customer success investment. It's also important to understand that the additional revenue delivered in this example will come much less expensively than new customer acquisition because there's no associated marketing expense and almost certainly less sales expense, too.

Improve the customer experience and customer satisfaction. Adam Miller is the CEO of Cornerstone OnDemand, an extremely successful recurring revenue company. He told me recently that he does not try to justify his significant investment in customer success financially. He believes so passionately in delivering on the company's value promise to its customers—and customer success is his vehicle for doing so—that he simply builds the cost of that team into his gross margin model and then manages to it. Financial results almost certainly accrue to Cornerstone from its customer success investment, but it's not the driving reason for doing so.

There's also something commonly referred to as *second-order revenue* that results from keeping and delighting customers. Most companies are not measuring and accounting for this in their financial models; it simply shows up as additional sales. But it's the direct result of customer success. Jason Lemkin, ex-CEO of Adobe Echosign, coined the phrase *second-order revenue* and attributes an increase of as much as 50 to 100 percent of the LTV of a customer to it. The theory is simple and logical:

- John loves your product and leaves Company A to join Company B and buys your product again at Company B.
- John loves your product and tells three friends about it and some of them end up buying your product, too.

Those two situations are actually quite measurable, and you should strive to do so. But there are a number of other positive effects of creating attitudinal loyalty—references, positive reviews, word-of-mouth, and so on. Real customer delight can be viral, too.

Customer Success Is a Fundamental Organizational Change

As mentioned in Chapter 1, real organizational change at the highest level in an enterprise is actually pretty rare. Although reorganizations are a way of life for most businesspeople, the fundamental org structure of a business has not changed much over the years:

- Somebody designs the product.
- Somebody builds the product.
- Somebody creates demand for the product.
- Somebody sells the product.
- Somebody installs/fixes the product.
- Somebody counts the money.

In the past 40 years, there has been only one major change to that standard organization model—the addition of IT. No business operates today without a deep dependence on technology, and that dependency necessitated the creation of an organization to manage that technology. This means that most companies today have a high-level org chart that looks like the one below (see Figure 2.1).

For all the reasons we've already explored in Chapter 1, customer success has now entered the landscape. It's not just a new title given to someone taking a different angle on an old job. That happens all the time. But

Figure 2.1   High-Level Organizational Chart

new organizations are different. They form only when some critical set of drivers come together, and usually one or more of those drivers is an external force affecting many or all companies. The formation of IT orgs to support the burgeoning technology explosion is a perfect example. It's happening now with customer success, too. Three key drivers must be present:

1. The business is dependent on it.
2. It requires a new set of skills to execute.
3. The activities and related metrics are new.

Business dependency. We spent all of Chapter 1 outlining how businesses have evolved to the point at which customer success is critical to the business. When you rely on customer LTV, not just a one-time sales event, to deliver long-term business success, it changes everything. People, technology, investment, and focus come to that part of the business, and one of the results is the formation of a new organization.

New skills. As with IT, customer success requires a new set of skills. You can't just take a smart engineer, make her a CIO, and expect her to manage all the technology in a company and understand the required processes, security, and administration to deliver the requisite business value. It's obviously not that simple. The same is true for customer success. If the business need for managing customer health does not exist, there's probably no one at your company who is analyzing the available data to determine which customers are healthy and which are not. There's also no one driving proactive outreach to customers who appear to need assistance or who have opportunities for growth. There may not even be anyone who knows how to measure churn, retention, customer growth, or customer satisfaction or which of those to even care about. The capabilities for doing this certainly exist, but they need to be turned into specific skills.

Activities and metrics. A big part of defining a new organization has to include defining what it will do and how it will be measured. Customer success certainly comes with the need for both. Someone has to decide what the key metrics are by which success will be determined:

- Gross renewals
- Net retention
- Adoption

- Customer health
- Churn
- Upsell
- Downsell
- Net Promoter Score (NPS)

And then the activities that will drive those metrics:

- Health checks
- Quarterly Business Reviews (QBRs)
- Proactive outreach
- Education/training
- Health scoring
- Risk assessment
- Risk mitigation processes

Some of those activities have been done in the past in critical situations and as one-offs, but, outside of a few mature SaaS companies, they have not been brought together and organized under one responsibility and with clear success metrics (see Figure 2.2).

Of course, it's not enough to just create a new box on an org chart even if you fill it with really smart people and give them the metrics by which they'll be measured and suggested activities for driving success. No organization stands alone, so let's discuss the keys to making this new organization work across the entire enterprise.

Let's start by getting on the same page with regard to terminology. *Customer success* is the term we're using in this book because it's the buzz

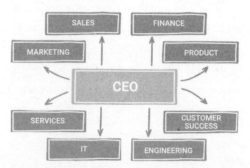

Figure 2.2 Expanded High-Level Organizational Chart

Figure 2.3 Organizing around Customer Success as a Philosophy

phrase that's caught on in the industry. But it's not the only term used to describe some kind of renewed focus on customers. There's not even consistency from one company to the next regarding what customer success means. As we mentioned in Chapter 1, customer success is a philosophy as well as a specific organization. As a philosophy, it often leads to an organization that looks like Figure 2.3.

You can see in this example that customer success is the umbrella phrase used to describe the entire post-sales world. It's a catchy, meaningful term because the goal for most companies really is to help make customers successful. Using it to describe the whole organization pushes that value front and center and sets the right expectations for both customers and employees. It's the kind of idea that CEOs and boards can get behind as they seek to become, or at least to be perceived as, more customer-centric.

You probably also noticed the box within the customer success organization labeled *Classic Customer Success*. I use that phrase to distinguish the philosophy of customer success from the part of the organization made up of people with that title who are actually the feet on the ground doing the hard work to drive success for their customers. I use the word *classic* because the original use of the term *customer success* at Salesforce, and many others after them, was to describe a very specific job and the department that was made up of people doing that job.

What Customer Success Is *Not*

As I mentioned, there are a number of other terms used to describe organizations or efforts within an enterprise that also bring more focus on the customer and are designed to improve the customer's experience and the value they get from their vendors. In most cases, these are not the same as customer success but may overlap in some areas, so it's important to understand them if you are going to understand customer success. Because of the buzz around customer success, the visibility of these organizations or efforts has also been raised, which has created some confusion in the market.

Customer experience (CX): CX typically refers to the assessment and management of the overall customer experience across a customer's lifetime. This includes understanding and managing the customer's experience at every touchpoint with the vendor from sales to onboarding to invoicing to customer support to renewals and is usually driven or measured by survey results. Many companies, such as Satmetrix, have successfully built their entire business around CX. It's a discipline that includes technology solutions, best practices, and conferences. Because customer satisfaction surveys are often part of measuring overall customer health, there is a tiny bit of overlap between customer success and customer experience.

Customer relationship management (CRM): CRM is widely used to describe the market space for solutions such as Salesforce.com, Microsoft Dynamics, Oracle CRM (Siebel Systems), and so on. In fact, Salesforce's stock market ticker symbol is CRM. It's a term primarily used to describe the market, not a specific role or discipline, but, because it's so ubiquitous, it is often viewed as subsuming customer success or that customer success is simply an offshoot of CRM. Customer success management could very accurately be called CRM if that term was not already in use to describe something very different. But in today's landscape, they are most certainly not one and the same.

Customer advocacy: Customer advocacy is used most often to describe the critical role that happy and successful customers can play in advancing a vendor's agenda with references, case studies, positive reviews, and user group participation. Industry, science, and technology solutions such as Influitive are being built around the idea of customer advocacy, and it is parallel and complementary to customer success. If customer success can be defined as managing customer health, then customer advocacy is a source of health-related data to assess one aspect of customer health. Customer advocacy may also be the output of those customers who have high health scores. You can see that customer success and customer advocacy might easily form a virtuous cycle.

Customer Success Is NOT Customer Support

There's one other critical organizational distinction that we should spend a few minutes discussing as it pertains to customer success and that is customer support. Customer support is an organization and discipline that has been around for a long time. The description of what customer support does almost always centers on the phrase *break/fix*. This is the 800-number, chat window, or e-mail address you use to get help with something that appears to be broken or not working as you expected. This touchpoint is critical to a customer's overall experience with a vendor. How many times have you heard someone complain about the long wait on hold or the unhelpful person they finally talked to? For many of us as customers, especially consumers, this is the primary point of contact with our vendors. That's one of the reasons that CX folks focus a lot of attention here. It's also a source of tremendous confusion when it comes to discussing customer success for a number of reasons.

One reason is that they sound similar, not just the words and the acronym CS but the perceived meaning. Isn't customer success just the new-age way of saying customer support? The answer is no, but that conclusion is an easy one to come to.

There's also usually an overlap in skills. Customer support people are expected to be product experts, as are Customer Success Managers. Both roles require good customer-facing skills (personality, patience, true desire to help, thick skin, etc.). Problem solving is also a useful talent in both roles.

Another source of confusion is simply naive logic, which usually goes like this: "If we have a team of people who know our product and help our customers when they need it, why do we need a second team of people with those same skills basically doing the same thing?"

To create a successful customer success organization requires that the lines of responsibility between them and customer support be drawn very clearly. There are several criteria that can help distinguish the two groups:

	Customer Success	**Customer Support**
Financial	Revenue-driver	Cost center
Action	Proactive	Reactive
Metrics	Success-oriented	Efficiency-oriented
Model	Analytics-focused	People-intensive
Goal	Predictive	Responsive

The two teams are not variations on a common theme and are actually paradoxical in many of the most important ways.

Too often, because of the similarities, customer success is initially formed inside the support organization. For all of the clear distinctions listed previously, this does not typically lead to success. What usually happens is that customer success becomes a type of premium support offering. Enhanced support offerings are a very good thing, but they aren't customer success. They typically offer positive elements for customers such as improved service-level agreements (SLAs), extended hours of support, multigeography support, designated points-of-contact, direct access to Level 2 support, and so forth. These are all very good things for which customers should, and do, pay extra, but they are still not customer success. They are primarily reactive to incoming customer problems and will ultimately be driven by efficiency (number of cases closed/day/rep). In contrast, customer success uses data to proactively predict and avoid customer challenges and will usually be measured by retention rates.

Both organizations are 100 percent needed to be effective as a company. The admonition here is simply to be mindful that they are not designed to accomplish the same goals and that organizational separation is actually far better than organizational proximity. Ultimately, the two teams will work closely together and actively collaborate on many customer situations, but the separation is required, at least initially, to formalize the discipline and processes around customer success without the influence of the reactive customer support team.

What Customer Success Is

Now that I hope we've cleared up some potential confusion, it's time to go beyond the simple org structure and talk about how to make a customer success–centric enterprise really work. A good place to start might be to elaborate on the criteria mentioned earlier that differentiate success from support. This might also help you understand the kind of person you will need to lead the organization and the characteristics of those filling the individual contributor roles as well.

Customer success is:

A revenue driver—Managing the installed base at a recurring revenue business means being responsible for a significant portion of the financial well-being of the company. Customer success is an organization that drives revenue in two ways.

1. Renewals (or avoidance of churn)—The renewal is a sales transaction whether it is explicit (signing a contract) or implicit (auto-renewal or non-opt out). As consumers, we live in this world with our cell-phone providers. Opting out at any given time is an option available to us. If we're under a two-year contract, there might be a penalty, but it's still an option. If we are not under any kind of contract, then we can opt out at any time without penalty. In either case, there is an implied sale that happens every month we don't change providers. The team responsible for ensuring that we don't opt out is what we're generally referring to as customer success in this book and what many B2B companies literally call customer success. Consumer companies such as AT&T or Verizon may not call it customer success, but there are certainly teams that analyze the data and try to avoid or mitigate the risks they identify in any given customer or group of customers.

2. Upsells—This is the act of buying more product from your vendor. To extend our cell-phone analogy, this happens when you buy a more expensive package, such as unlimited international calling or unlimited text messaging or more data. Those are upsells that increase the value of your contract to your provider. The same thing happens in the B2B world.

In many cases, the customer success team may not actually execute on the sales transaction, whether it's a renewal or an upsell. There are often specific sales teams for contract negotiations and for final signatures. But, even if the sales transactions are not executed by customer success, they are enabled by them. To repeat something we've said before, successful customers do two things: (1) remain customers (renewing their contract or not opting out) and (2) buy more stuff from you. Because the job of customer success is to make sure customers are deriving success from your product, they are a revenue-driving organization. This means they need to be people who are at least sales-savvy, if not having direct sales experience.

Proactive—This is a major difference from customer support in which most individuals react to incoming customer requests, whether they are phone calls, chat requests, e-mails, or tweets. Customer success teams use data and analytics to determine which customers should be acted on, either because they appear to be at risk or because there appears to be an upsell opportunity or because there's a regularly scheduled event such as a QBR. Beware of bringing into customer success those who have spent their lives being reactive. The transition is doable but is a tough one.

Success oriented—Success metrics drive top-line (bookings or revenue) financial gains for your company. New business sales is clearly a success metric. In the customer success world, the key metrics are often renewal rates, upsell percentages, overall growth of your customer base, and so forth. Efficiency metrics are very different from these. They are focused on reducing costs as opposed to increasing revenue. Cutting the assembly time for a new car by one day is an efficiency metric. If you build a lot of cars, this is tremendously valuable to the company but does not directly result in the sale of more cars. People who are efficiency experts are not necessarily the same people who will successfully drive more revenue or bookings.

Analytics-focused—Most businesses and organizations are driven by analytics, but customer success is driven by forward-looking, or predictive, analytics in a way that many others are not. The sales analogy here is to analytics that help you identify the best opportunities in your pipeline upon which to act. Analytics similarly drive customer success by predicting outcomes such as churn or upsell, allowing the optimization of the time spent by the team. Time spent by an expert with a happy customer will usually yield good things, such as higher customer satisfaction scores and more references. But that may not be as valuable as time spent with a struggling customer that ensures their retention. Being analytics-focused with the right kind of predictive data is critical to driving an effective customer success team.

Predictive—This needs to be the customer success focus, not only of the analytics and actual analysis but also of the people. Remember the contrasting position is simply responsiveness. It's a great thing to improve your responsiveness, especially when it comes to customers. They appreciate it, and it makes for a better overall experience for both parties. But predictability takes this one step further—figuring out who to talk to before they need to call you.

Customer Success's Cross-Functional Impact

In creating good overall organizational health with the insertion of this new team, the first thing that needs to be recognized is that customer success is not a philosophy isolated to the organization by the same name. It must become an idea that permeates the entire company and culture. Perhaps more than any other organization, customer success is not an island. Regardless of whether you run a recurring revenue business, if you are truly committed to the success of your customers as a primary pillar of your business, every part of your company must be equally committed to it and incented by it.

Let's consider incentives for a moment. One way to ensure that all parts of your company are truly committed to customer success is to apply appropriate incentives. Most companies have an executive bonus plan, and many also have a bonus plan that goes down to most, if not all, employees. In both cases, the bonus is probably tied to overall company success. That means someone, probably your CEO with board approval, decides what the right measures of company success are and what the appropriate payouts are, too. At some companies, it might be just based on sales growth. At others, it could be profitability. At a customer success–driven company, it will include some kind of retention metric, too. A simple, but extremely effectively plan might have only two elements—top-line revenue/bookings growth (sales) and retention. If every employee, but especially the executives, were equally incented to be thinking about retention and sales, that sends a very strong statement that the company prioritizes both, and has a high likelihood of accomplishing what compensation/bonus plans are usually designed to do—change behavior.

Another related idea here is to ensure that one person is the owner of the customer success metric, which might be a renewal rate, a net retention rate, or a customer satisfaction score. Whatever the measure, one person needs to own it. There's an old business saying that's very true: "If many people own something, no one owns it." You wouldn't think of running a business and not having one person responsible for the sales number, right? If you are committing to customer success as an equivalent pillar (to sales) in the long-term success of your company, don't you need to do the same thing with your retention number? Most definitely. Assign it to someone and give her the same authority that you give to your sales vice president

(VP) to make his number. The authority to shake trees, push on other organizations, fight for resources, make strategic business decisions, or all of the above. Someone needs to own it and know that his job depends on making his number. One could easily argue that the primary job of the leader of your customer success efforts is to ensure that all other organizations are consistently thinking about retention.

These two ideas come together to drive a healthy business forward in the following way. Joe is the VP of sales at Acme. Acme has been around for a while and is a healthy, growing business. He has 45 quota-carrying sales reps, 15 solution consultants, and 5 more staff to run the order desk, administer the tools they use, and generally support the team. He also carries a $73 million bookings quota for this year. Joe obviously reports to the CEO.

On the other side of the office is Sherrie. Sherrie is the VP of customer success. She has 29 CSMs, 7 renewal and upsell reps, and 3 people in customer success operations supporting her and the team. She's responsible for managing all 2,200 Acme customers. She carries a $145 million bookings quota for this year. That's $132 million of renewals and a 10 percent upsell target for an overall net retention goal of 110 percent. She also reports directly to the CEO.

One thing I'm sure you noticed is that Sherrie's number is larger than the VP of sales. Significantly larger. This happens in a recurring revenue business, and it often does not take long—four to five years for a healthy, growing company and shorter if the top-line starts to flatten. Consider a company that started three years ago and did $1 million, $4 million, and $10 million of bookings in those three years. Let's also say that net retention has been 100 percent so far, meaning the current value of the installed base (ARR) is $15 million. Now let's assume that the growth target for sales for the coming year is 50 percent. This is a nice, not-uncommon company story and a reasonably aggressive growth strategy. It also means that whoever owns retention, assuming net retention will be 110 percent going forward, will have a bigger target than the VP of sales: $16.5 million versus $15 million in the coming year. That difference will grow quickly over time. If both hit their number this year and the same growth targets exist the following year, the numbers will be $34.7 million and $22.5 million, respectively. See Figure 2.4 for how their respective quotas will look over several years.

Back to our story. On a Monday morning Joe walks into the office of the VP of engineering, which he does several times a week. The conversation

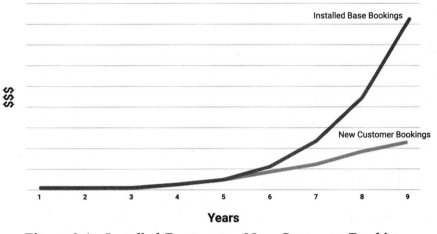

Years

Figure 2.4   Installed Base versus New Customer Bookings

likely centers around the things Joe needs from Bill to make his number this year.

"The competition is killing us on a couple of missing features, and an integration with WhatBit would give us a competitive advantage I could sell the heck out of. Plus, I need a little hack on our demo, probably no more than two to three days of work, to make it really rock." Parting words may go like this, "If we can't get these things done, we'll have a really tough time making our sales number, and we'll all get killed as stockholders."

This kind of conversation happens all the time and has for years.

Later that same day, Sherrie also walks into Bill's office. The ensuing conversation actually sounds pretty similar but, of course, with Sherrie's twist on it.

"Overall performance is really hurting us right now. A couple of key customers are putting some pressure on their renewal as a result. Also, there's a report that I know looks ugly in a demo, but our customers are screaming for it. One other thing—the Blart feature is really cool, but I need it to stand alone so we can sell it as an upgrade, not part of the standard package. If we can make these things happen, I think I have a shot at my number, and we'll all be happier stockholders."

The problem is clear, right? These requests compete with each other. Both are good for the business; nevertheless, there's tension as a result. Tension is nothing new in a business. Organizational tension, if managed properly, is the engine that drives a company forward. The previous scenario is why you want Bill, the VP of engineering, to be both incented and influenced equally by his conversations with Joe and Sherrie. As the CEO, you need to create this reality. Joe and Sherrie each own a number that's critical to your business. You want them to have equal authority around the company to make their number so the business will thrive. You also want Bill to be incented to deliver for both of them. Sherrie's conversation needs to have the same weight with Bill as Joe's conversation does. This is a power shift at most companies. Sales is king, and has been forever, and rightly so. When top-line growth is the only thing that really matters, the person driving those results has the power. But when you turn your focus as a company toward customer success, especially if you are a recurring revenue business, some of that power will move to the person who owns retention. Over time, as your installed base becomes far more valuable than new business bookings, the power shift will continue accordingly.

Impact on Sales

Now, let's take a closer look at each of the major organizational groups within an enterprise and how a customer success focus will change how they operate. Because we've already started down this path, let's start with sales.

I'm actually going to lump sales and marketing together here as their joint goal is the same. I'll narrow marketing down, for the purposes of this discussion, to demand generation—the people and processes that feed leads to the sales team to drive new customer acquisition. How does this world change if the company is newly focused on customer success and retention? Several things will happen either immediately or over time:

1. A new focus on marketing and selling only to customers who can be successful long-term with your product
2. Less emphasis on maximizing the initial deal, especially if it's at the expense of LTV
3. Overall awareness of renewals
4. Improved expectation-setting with prospects
5. Much more attention paid to knowledge-transfer and post-sales prep to ensure onboarding and ongoing success for the customer
6. Incentives around renewals and/or LTV

These are significant and fundamental shifts in the thinking of your acquisition team. Similar to CEOs, as discussed in Chapter 1, sales reps really do want customers to have long-term success. Most are not out to simply make their money at the expense of the rest of the company. But again, their incentives and a history of short-term thinking often get in the way. For your company to have long-term success, the way you think about demand generation and sales and perhaps how they are incented may need to dramatically change.

At the extreme, you may even end up giving veto power over sales deals to the person who owns retention. This sounds like a dangerous proposition, and it is. But it might be the right thing to do if the power is wielded very carefully and driven by real data, not just anecdotes and instincts. Ultimately, if this authority is not given to your VP of customer success or to the chief customer officer, it resides in your lap as the CEO and the one who has to balance the need to make this quarter's number with the pain of selling to the wrong customer and possibly even losing that customer in the long run.

Over time, and with the accumulation and analysis of lots of data, these decisions should be information-driven, even to the point of refocusing your demand generation team on only those prospects who have a high likelihood of a lifetime of success.

Impact on Product

Now, let's talk about your product team. I'm encompassing both product management and engineering/development/manufacturing in this discussion. We've already examined one example in our story of Joe, Sherrie, and Bill. Because customers are no longer held captive by the enormity of the upfront investment and the cost of change, your product thinking must also shift toward retention, not just sales. To put it simply, your product must deliver to customers just as much as it appeals to prospects. In fact, one definition of customer success that I've heard is *delivering on the sales promise*. Remember that the shift here is not only about caring about customers but also about knowing that their LTV is life or death for your company. Retention thinking in your product team might look like this:

- Building return on investment (ROI) measurements into your product
- Making your product easier to implement

- Designing for ease of adoption, not just functionality
- Stickiness is more important than features
- Performance is more valuable than demo quality
- Creating modules that can be upsold rather than integrating all features into the base package
- Making customer self-sufficiency easier to attain

Many of those characteristics are part of the natural thinking of a great product team already, but customer success–centric companies will make them imperatives, not nice-to-haves.

The good news is that, in a properly organized, customer-focused business, the person who owns retention or customer satisfaction will constantly drive these imperatives. No one needs to remind everyone at a company how important it is to be able to sell your product to new customers. But it's new thinking to bring retention and LTV into the same focus for much of the company. Not so for your VP of customer success who will have this in her DNA. No one will need to remind her how important customers are. Her paycheck and job will be riding on it, and she will, if she's doing her job well, consistently refocus the entire company in this direction.

Impact on Services

For your services team, the shift in thinking is a bit more subtle. It's really much more about urgency for them than it is specific line items such as we listed earlier. I like to boil it down to one statement: "In a recurring revenue business, there's no such thing as post-sales. Every single activity is a pre-sales activity."

Contrast the urgency in implementing your software for a customer who is on a quarterly contract versus one who purchased a perpetual license. In the latter case, a project miss of two to three days or even a week probably doesn't matter that much. But for the customer who will have a decision point in 90 days (60 working days) on whether to keep your product, two to three days can make a huge difference.

Across the entire services team, this must be the mentality. The person taking a customer support call needs to think of the resolution of that problem as a pre-sales activity. Sales reps and solution consultants view every interaction with a customer as critical because the clock is ticking on the current month/quarter/year, and they need to get this deal closed. Customer support reps need to take on that same urgency. Resolving this problem for this customer as quickly as possible is mandatory because of the impending deal that could be hanging in the balance. That impending deal, of course, is the renewal or the opportunity to churn if there isn't a formal renewal or, in the case of a pay-as-you-go business, the opportunity to create a need for more of your product.

One of the jobs of a great CSM is to always be asking the question, "Why does this customer need my help right now? What could we do or what should we have done differently upstream so I would not be needed for this task?" This thinking often results in putting pressure on other parts of the services business:

- Customer support didn't adequately resolve a problem.
- A critical case is open for too long in customer support.
- The customer went through the training for how to build reports but does not understand how to build the reports they need.
- The configuration that the onboarding team did does not solve the use case the customer needs solved.

In all of these cases, the job of customer success (the CSM or her management) is not just to help get the customer over that challenge but to go to the source and apply pressure to ensure that the next customer does not end up in the same situation. This means going back to support or training or onboarding, forcing them to step up their game. Clearly, the best customer experience is not to have someone who can help when needed but needing that help less and less frequently.

To be fair, the same requirement exists for customer success to go back and challenge the non–services organizations when they've set the customer up for failure, too:

- Sales set the wrong expectations about what the product can do.
- The product does not function as promised.

But a large portion of the organizational influence that will allow customer success to deliver true success to your customers will take place within the services organization. That's why the urgency with which services approaches every task and challenge is paramount. They must begin to think of themselves as pre-sales people, not post-sales.

This is yet another reason why the VP of customer success must have real authority and possess true leadership qualities. So much of what she does to move your company forward has to do with influencing others who do not work for her. She needs to have the gravitas, incentive, and skills to go toe-to-toe with the VP of sales or the VP of engineering or the leaders of any of the other organizations. In many ways, the right customer success leader will bear a striking resemblance in skill set to your VP of sales with a little bit more of a service orientation instead of a closing mentality.

3 | Customer Success for Traditional Nonrecurring Revenue Businesses

Today, customer success is largely centered in the world of B2B SaaS companies. As we've discussed, it's the urgency created by the subscription model that has driven the need for customer success and placed it into the business consciousness. But, does it apply to other businesses as well?

The answer is a resounding, *yes*. The need for customer success concepts, by any name, is being discovered and, in some cases, rediscovered by many B2C and non-technology companies for a variety of reasons including:

1. Most companies are thinking about how to become a subscription-based business or at least create some subscription-based products.
2. Creating great customer experiences and ensuring that customers derive true business value from your products pays off. Even in a nonsubscription business, repeat business is key. If you live in a world where that's true, then consider how customer success can help you.

Remember that the phrase *customer success* is simply another way of saying *loyalty creation* and especially *attitudinal loyalty creation*. In businesses in which physical customer success teams exist, they exist to drive loyalty, which results in retention and revenue growth. Loyal customers stay with you and buy more from you. Every company wants their customers to do both of those things. Subscriptions have become step one in the process for doing just that, which is why, with the help of technology, they are exploding into every market. But subscriptions aren't the Holy Grail; they are merely the starting point. With every subscription comes the reality that we've handed much of the power over to the customer, and that means you must deliver what they need or want in order to get your desired business results. That's where customer success comes in, whether that's a team of people intervening directly with your customers or technology helping you deliver relevant and timely messages to them to make their experience better.

Are Subscriptions Only for Software and Magazines?

Let's start by looking at the expansion of the subscription economy beyond software because it's such a key element in the growth and importance of customer success. There are subscriptions that have been around for years and that we're accustomed to:

- Magazines
- Fitness centers
- Cable TV
- Country clubs
- Traditional technology (hardware/software maintenance)

Newer ones we're rapidly adopting:

- Movies (Netflix)
- Satellite radio (SiriusXM)
- Music (Pandora, Spotify, Apple Music)
- Diet programs (Nutrisystem, Weight Watchers)
- HSA plans (all major insurance carriers)
- Grocery delivery (Instacart)

And those that have yet to change our lives but may soon:

- Razors (Dollar Shave Club)
- Meals (Blue Apron, EAT Club)

- Health drinks (Soylent)
- Package delivery (Amazon Prime)
- Prescriptions (PillPack)
- Fitness centers V2 (ClassPass)

Every business in the world is thinking about how to become subscription based. You don't think Starbucks execs are talking about the right price for an unlimited coffee subscription? If it's less than $50 per month, you can count me in. And what about a company like Uber? You can bet there are teams of data scientists combing through the numbers and trying to come up with an Uber subscription—all the rides you want in San Francisco for $225 a month, maybe? That would stop a lot of people from taking the occasional taxi or using Lyft when that might be slightly more convenient. These programs are supremely powerful because they deliver two things that every company craves and loves: predictable revenue and loyalty. Both of those concepts are bidirectional, too. As customers, we tend to love predictable expenses just as businesses love predictable revenue. That's why many consumers choose to pay the same amount to their power company every month instead of worrying about the highs and lows caused by seasonality. The other point is a bit more subtle, but human nature bends toward loyalty as a positive thing, even a badge of honor. Have you ever heard a conversation between a Ford truck owner and a Chevy truck owner? Loyalty to the point of fisticuffs in some parts of the world. We just want to be proud of the decisions we've made, which means our loyalty is there for the taking, and a subscription model is the perfect device for taking and servicing that desire for loyalty.

The concepts mentioned previously have been in place and building loyalty for years, from any company that offers a frequent flyer/shopper program. By definition, companies that offer these programs are in the pay-as-you-go business, and, as we mentioned earlier, pay-as-you-go looks very much like a subscription business when it comes to managing customers. Frequent shopper programs offer all sorts of reasons for you to continue to do your business with one company, forsaking all others. When I rent a car these days, it's always from National Car Rental. They have all my information, allow me to walk straight to where the cars are, select the one I want, and drive to the exit, where all I have to do is show my driver's license. Amazingly convenient compared with the nonmember process, which includes lines, forms, and lots of initials and signatures. Now that I'm locked in, it's highly unlikely I'd rent from another company unless they found a way to make my life even easier, such as delivering my rental to the exit where I'll be coming out of the airport and letting me drop it off where I want to.

The *frequent x* industry that first comes to mind is obviously the airlines with their frequent-flyer programs. As I was pondering the writing of this book, a friend of mine asked me whether customer success was applicable outside of SaaS. My knee-jerk response was, "not really." But then he challenged me with a simple question: "What happens when the United flight you are scheduled to be on later today is delayed?" The answer: I get a text message informing me of the delay and either the new estimated time of departure or the expected time of the next update. Isn't that customer success? United Airlines certainly wants me to fly on its planes as often as possible. Because air travel is anything but a perfect experience, part of what United needs to do to be successful is to keep me informed when things are not going according to plan. Thus, the text message when a flight is delayed, when a gate change takes place, or informing me where my luggage is when it didn't get on the same flight as me.

Much of the daily job of the CSM in a SaaS company has to do with setting and resetting customer expectations, too. The new release that was planned to ship on Thursday is now delayed two weeks. The reporting feature the customer wanted has now slipped into the October release. Or, on the positive side, the premium support program we've promised is available starting today, not September 1 as we originally planned. All of these are part of what CSMs do every day and are analogous to what United Airlines is doing when they keep me informed and my expectations realistic. And these outreaches are part of an improved customer experience, which leads to retention in the same way that the perks of the frequent-flyer program do. It's all part of the customer journey, and the core philosophy of customer success is simply to maximize the value the customer receives from your product(s) to keep them coming back. This idea clearly crosses over from B2B SaaS to nontechnology companies and to B2C companies.

Let's look at one more example of the world moving toward a subscription model. Did you know that Volkswagen is now a SaaS company? It's true. In their new vehicles, they are shipping Apple's CarPlay functionality standard. That's not really news as lots of auto companies are doing that with either CarPlay or Android Auto. What is new is that Volkswagen has extended CarPlay with its own set of Car-Net applications, which will allow you access to features such as remote lock control, remote honk and flash, parking information, stolen vehicle location, automatic crash notifications, diagnostics, and vehicle monitoring. And here's where it becomes SaaS: CarPlay is standard, but the Volkswagen-specific Car-Net apps are an upgrade that costs $199 per year. Did you catch that last part? Per year! The birth of another SaaS company—shipping software for which a monthly or annual fee is required. And that's surely just the beginning. It's not much of a stretch to imagine a car company offering a subscription-based vehicle ownership program. For $650 a month, you can choose from any of 15 car models that you'd like to drive, and you can switch cars, within your allocated plan, whenever you like. Because software is eating (and connecting) the world, each car you choose will be delivered to you with your radio stations preprogrammed, your seat preferences preset, and your temperature controls exactly the way you like them. In addition, your registration and insurance will be digitally accessible from the car's software and displayable on screen to any police officer to whom you wish to show them. And then those car companies will be looking to hire you, the readers of this book, in a desperate attempt to find customer success expertise as it will be required in a whole new way for them to be successful.

And there's not a business that won't be affected by these changes. If car companies, prescription providers, and over-the-air radio are all moving toward subscriptions, is there any doubt that every business will at least try to do the same? It's a way to create or ensure loyalty and to expand your business, making it more accessible to customers who otherwise might not have been in your target market.

Delivering Customer Success

Although the customer success philosophy is basically the same, there are some major differences with regard to how it is delivered by different companies. Here are three examples with rough estimates of customers and ASPs:

1. Workday—hundreds of customers at $1 million/year
2. Clarizen—thousands of customers at $15,000/year
3. Netflix—millions of customers at $10/month

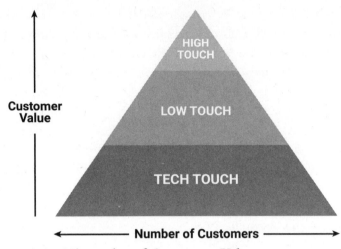

Figure 3.1   Hierarchy of Customer Value

It's pretty obvious that these three companies cannot manage customer success in the same way. Workday can afford to throw some bodies at their customers, such as product and domain experts who can spend significant time helping customers to understand and effectively use their products. Clarizen can do the same with certain customers but also needs to worry about scaling for the long tail of lower value customers it wants to keep. Netflix can do nothing with its customers that isn't 100 percent automated. No phone calls or meetings ever happen regularly between a Netflix CSM and a customer. There's clearly a hierarchy of customer value here and an associated touch model for each level. For many companies, this model can be applied to their entire customer base, with different customers falling into each of the three categories (see Figure 3.1).

Let's examine more closely what customer success looks like at each tier in the pyramid. Understanding this is essential in visualizing how customer success applies to every business regardless of size and regardless of the size of their customers.

High touch. This model is, by definition, the most people-intensive, but that expense is justified by the price the customer is paying for the product. This model is most commonly deployed in SaaS companies, such as Workday, that have customers paying significant amounts of money for their products. However, it's not exclusive to SaaS by any means. Think about a contract between DIRECTV and Marriott to provide television options to every room in every Marriott hotel worldwide. You can bet there's someone at DIRECTV responsible for managing that critical business relationship and who has significant authority for getting things done across every organization in the company in order to satisfy such an important customer. That's customer success regardless of what it's called—driving loyalty by delivering value.

The high-touch model often consists of frequent interactions, some scheduled, some not, between the vendor and customer. Great high-touch customer success is usually a predefined mixture of the scheduled and unscheduled. Typical scheduled interactions might include:

- A defined onboarding process
- Coordinated handoffs between vendor groups
- Monthly status meetings
- Executive business reviews (EBRs; biannually or quarterly)
- On-site visits (might be very frequent or annually)
- Regular health checks
- Upcoming renewal (if subscription based)

Unscheduled interactions are usually data driven and proactive from the vendor to the customer and designed to mitigate a perceived risk:

- Multiple outages
- Too many customer support/customer service calls
- Declining usage of the product
- Invoices overdue by more than X days

One thing you'll notice about unscheduled interactions is that they would probably compel action on the part of the vendor whether they are operating in a high-touch model or a tech-touch model. You can imagine alarm bells going off at Netflix if a previously prolific customer suddenly went 60 days without requesting a movie. That wouldn't stimulate a phone call to the customer but might very well start an e-mail campaign or initiate the sending of some kind of automated reminder.

In the high-touch model, all of these interactions are probably personal, whether phone calls or face-to-face. The key challenge is to optimize the customer touches to create maximum benefit for the associated cost. And because the associated costs are people-heavy, they tend to be relatively very expensive. This expense is a reasonable cost of doing business with customers who are paying hundreds of thousands of dollars a year (or more) for your products, but they still need to be optimized to deliver maximum business benefit for both the customer and the vendor.

For the vendor, this is obviously a critical business process because the high-touch model is typically applied only to your most valuable customers: customers whose loss would be catastrophic not only financially but also in many other ways. The application of expensive resources in a high-touch model usually has a very simple retention goal—100.00 percent. Anything less is most likely a major failure. The customers who receive this high-touch treatment are also often those with great opportunity for expansion. Think back to the hypothetical DIRECTV and Marriott relationship. What are the odds that Marriott will build or acquire more hotels? Highly likely, right? Every new room results in additional dollars for DIRECTV if they keep Marriott happy. It's a long-term play that goes beyond 100 percent retention but is expected to grow the value of that relationship financially over time, too.

It's pretty easy to see how high-touch customer success applies in nontechnology and B2C businesses just as it does in B2B SaaS. In the DIRECTV/Marriott example, DIRECTV is primarily a B2C company but clearly with a set of customers who force them to operate as a B2B vendor. Marriott wouldn't be the only customer fitting that bill either. Any sports bar chain, such as Buffalo Wild Wings, that wants to provide every possible sporting event on one of their 35 big screens at every one of their locations, will look a lot like Marriott from a relationship standpoint. DIRECTV is not alone in dealing with this challenge (or opportunity). Many businesses, perhaps most, do not fit cleanly into one model or the other. Dropbox is another company that started as a pure B2C play, but once they realized that many of the consumers using their application worked for the same companies, they began to think about B2B and enterprise and have now become a vendor serving both businesses and consumers.

A nontechnology company that knows a little something about high-touch customer success is Bright Horizons. If you have kids and work for a large company, you may know who they are. Bright Horizons provides childcare options to large companies who want to include that as part of their employees' benefits package. As you can imagine, these contracts with major employers are critical for Bright Horizons. So they have a team of people who manage those relationships with the intention of delivering high levels of retention and growing those relationships financially. Growth happens through upselling other capabilities that Bright Horizons can offer such as backup childcare, educational services, and even eldercare. As you can see, because of the subscription nature of both businesses, Workday and Bright Horizons provide high-touch customer success to their customers with the same intentions:

- **Product adoption**: Workday wants customers to use their software and get real value from it. Bright Horizons wants the employees of their customers to use their services to make their lives better.
- **Customer satisfaction**: great references sell in every business. There's nothing like good word-of-mouth to spread the word about a product or service that really works. And there's nothing like customer testimonials to enhance your sales process.
- **Upsell**: successful and happy customers buy more stuff from you. That's just the way it works. If you have more products and services to offer, your best customers are your most likely buyers and the cost of sales to them is massively smaller.
- **Retention**: this is always at the core of customer success. Driving loyalty, not just for the sake of loyalty and warm, fuzzy feelings, but because it's a business imperative if you run a recurring revenue business.

In many ways, the high-touch model is the easiest to staff, deploy, and execute. People and companies have been doing high-touch account management forever, so it's not hard to find people with the right customer-facing skills and brainpower to figure out how to deliver success to their customers. It's primarily a relationship job enhanced with business savvy. But don't think that technology doesn't play a role here. It most certainly does. But the role of technology for high-touch models is primarily about communication, collaboration, and management and not so much about automation or optimizing who to touch and when. We'll discuss technology in more detail in a later chapter.

Low touch. As you can imagine, the low-touch customer success model is a blend of the high-touch and tech-touch models, combining elements of each. The low-touch model is for those *tweener* customers, not quite big enough or strategic enough to warrant the white-glove treatment of the high-touch customers but important enough that you are willing to do some level of one-on-one touch with them. As with any three-tier model, the middle tier inevitably becomes the *mushy middle* creating fuzzy lines both at the top and at the bottom. But dividing lines must be drawn no matter how thin the line might be between the least valuable high-touch customer and the most valuable low-touch customer and similarly at the bottom of the tier.

If you are not a pure tech-touch company, which many B2C companies have to be, then you'll almost certainly have a tier of customers that can accurately be defined as low touch. One way to think about the model for managing these customers is just-in-time customer success.

Just-in-time is a phrase I've stolen here from the world of manufacturing. It's also often referred to as the Toyota Production System (TPS) because it was pioneered in Toyota manufacturing plants in the 1960s. Early in the days of mass production manufacturing, huge warehouses were required to stock the inventory of parts and materials required by the manufacturing line to build the products that had been sold or committed. Those warehouses and that inventory were extremely expensive parts of the process. The combination of smart businesspeople looking to save money along with the improvement in ordering and transportation systems allowed companies to reduce the amount of inventory they kept on hand by having it delivered much closer to the time of actual need. In a perfect system, the part that the assembly-line person needs to put on the car she is building arrives at the station just as she reaches for it, having come straight off the truck and never even stopping to be counted as inventory.

Customer success for low-touch customers can operate in a similar way, thus the stealing of the phrase just-in-time (JIT). JIT customer success means providing exactly what the customer needs at exactly the right time. Not a minute before or a minute after. These customers are not valuable enough for you to store inventory for them. Inventory in this case would be an abundance of guidance, education, or handholding, all of which also lead to something priceless—goodwill. In other words, JIT also means just enough. In the high-touch model, lots of inventory/goodwill is stored up because of the number of interactions that take place with each of those customers. It's worth going the extra mile and perhaps doing more than what is necessary because of the importance of these customers. In the low-touch model, you can't afford to do as many interactions, so you will end up driving toward the bare minimum. But, in this model, the bare minimum still includes a reasonable degree of one-on-one touch. By contrast, the tech-touch model removes one-on-one touch completely.

Not surprisingly, low touch starts to incorporate elements of tech-touch to complement the one-on-one touches. Let's revisit the set of scheduled touches that we defined for our high-touch model:

- A defined onboarding process
- Coordinated handoffs between vendor groups
- Monthly status meetings
- Executive business reviews (biannually or quarterly)
- On-site visits (might be very frequent or annually)
- Regular health checks
- Upcoming renewal (if subscription based)

In the low-touch model, many of these might still be relevant. You may completely eliminate some of them such as on-site visits, and you'll almost certainly change the frequency of most of them. A version of the above list updated for low-touch customers might then look like this:

- A ~~defined~~ packaged onboarding process
- Coordinated handoffs ~~between vendor groups~~ only from sales to onboarding
- ~~Monthly status meetings~~
- EBRs (~~bi-annually or quarterly~~ annually)
- ~~On-site visits (might be very frequent or annually)~~
- Regular *automated* health checks
- ~~Upcoming~~ Auto-renewal (if subscription based)

Similarly, the unscheduled touches would be carefully altered to minimize the expense. In this case, the thresholds might simply be raised (or lowered, depending on your point of view). For example, if more than 10 support/services requests in a 30-day period triggered an outreach for high-touch customers, maybe that number goes to 20 for low-touch customers. In addition, technology will come more into play as you can see for scheduled touches. Perhaps the first three outreaches for an invoice that's overdue are all e-mails, and then the first two one-on-one touches are performed by a junior finance person rather than a more expensive CSM.

It's obvious that the tiers and associated touch models are all about driving your business toward profitability or at least viability. In a healthy customer success–focused company, the tiers and touch models are well defined and are used as headcount drivers. If we look back at the high-touch model, it's fairly easy to estimate the amount of time it will take a CSM to prepare and perform each of the tasks and how often the unscheduled ones will occur. Taking into account that some portion of any CSM's time is going to be spent in internal meetings or doing non-customer-facing activities, you should be able to estimate the CSM time required each year/month/week with any given customer, which will in turn define how many customers a CSM can manage. Voila! Your headcount model.

Two quick comments here. (1) Your first pass at this is highly likely to show you the need for far more heads than your CFO or CEO will allow you to have. But at least you'll have a model you can tweak and around which you can have intelligent conversations about which tasks to eliminate or automate to reduce the headcount needs. (2) You'll find that the best way to determine CSM ratios is not by number of customers but by contract value (ARR). All customers are not created equal, so a $2 million per year customer can't be counted the same as a $20,000 per year customer. As a counterpoint, it's much harder to manage one hundred $20,000 customers than one $2 million customer, so keep that in mind, too.

Just as with the high-touch model, the low-touch model is fully applicable to many nontechnology and B2C businesses. Some B2C businesses, for example, have a surprisingly small target market and thus relatively small customer bases. That allows for the low-touch techniques we have just discussed to be applied in those situations. Tech-touch is not always the only option just because a company is primarily B2C.

One example of this type of company is Nipro Diagnostics. Among their many products is a self-monitoring blood glucose meter for home diabetes diagnostics. The consumer has to purchase the meter once and then replenish the test strips on a regular basis. The meter delivers the results to a mobile device using Bluetooth, and they can then be shared with the user's health-care provider. Home health care enabled by technology is a significant worldwide trend that is barely in its infancy. But the point of the story is that the glucose meter and the associated test strips, which can be delivered directly to your home, are simply a home health-care version of razors and blades. The need to replenish the user's supply of test strips on a regular basis makes this essentially a subscription model à la Dollar Shave

Club. And because the customer base is relatively small, the customer success model can be a combination of low touch and tech touch. Low touch is done through the health-care provider (channel partner) who helps the consumer understand how to use the product effectively and how consistent use provides great value to their overall health and peace of mind. Tech touch is done directly through the device delivering the results of each test to the user almost immediately. Effective customer success is a fundamental component of this business model, including the possibility of intervention if too much time lapses and the customer has not renewed his order of test strips. Nipro Diagnostics may know nothing about Silicon Valley's new secret sauce—customer success—but its business model demands an effective management of its customers, which ensures that Nipro delivers on the promise of its product. It matters not what they call it. A rose by any other name would smell as sweet.

Tech touch. This model may be the most complex and interesting of all. How do you deliver timely and relevant customer success to your customers without ever talking to them directly? Because the SaaS model lowers the barrier to entry for customers and the cost of sales for the vendor, it also broadens each market, often significantly. Ultimately, this almost always leads to a long tail of low-value customers. Individually, they do not have a lot of strategic or financial value, but, collectively, they often play a major role in the vendor's financial results. For the long tail, tech-touch customer success is a necessity. For most B2C companies, it's not just a necessity, it's the only choice.

Tech touch simply means that all customer touches are technology driven. Another way to say this is that all touches need to be one-to-many. One-to-one touches are far too expensive and clearly can't scale to handle the volumes of customers we're talking about. Oftentimes, a conversation about tech-touch centers on e-mail. Although e-mail is a powerful tool in the customer success arsenal for tech-touch customers, it's not the only tool. Other one-to-many channels exist, too, such as

- Webinars
- Podcasts
- Communities (online portals for sharing ideas and talking virtually to other customers)
- User groups
- Customer summits

Any vehicle that allows you to interact with more than one customer at a time, or moves those interactions to another source (Communities), is an option for executing customer success at scale. Let's explore e-mail in some depth as it's arguably the most powerful, offering the ability to be very timely, highly relevant, and information driven. E-mail marketing is also a well-understood discipline, and the technology behind it has been vetted and hardened over the past decade.

Targeted e-mail marketing has taken the world by storm over the past dozen years. Three providers of marketing automation software were successful enough to do an IPO—Eloqua, Marketo, and Hubspot. Two other software providers, focused primarily on the B2C world, Responsys and Exact Target, also did very successful IPOs. And each of those companies, at one point, achieved a market valuation in excess of $1 billion. That's clear proof that there was really some *there* there. The core concept of targeted e-mail marketing is pretty simple. Create smart e-mail campaigns based on demographic and behavioral knowledge of prospects to lead them down the buying path. These campaigns have become very sophisticated with complex branching logic and multichannel intelligence. However, it's all been aimed at the top of the funnel—customer acquisition. But the times, they are a-changin.'

Now targeted e-mail marketing is coming to customer success, and it applies the same concepts to customers (instead of prospects), helping them along the customer journey and leading them to successful use of your product. It's still demand generation at its core, but with a twist. For existing customers, it's about creating demand for the product they already own. Remember our euphemism for customer success—*building loyalty*. The goal of customer e-mail campaigns is not solely to get customers to buy more, although you will occasionally target customers for that purpose. It's to reinforce the purchase they've already made or help them use that product more effectively so that they remain loyal, either by renewing their contracts or choosing to not opt-out. The real power in using e-mail is that, once the infrastructure is in place, sending the e-mails is essentially free and highly scalable. For companies with large customer bases, this capability is a lifesaver because, although there are other one-to-many channels at their disposal, e-mail is the most effective. Let's dig into why that is the case.

Effective e-mails need to be timely, relevant, and include useful information. Similar to the marketing automation scenario described earlier for prospects, there is a lot of information available about customers that can be used to create highly effective e-mails. In fact, there is far more information available about customers than there is about prospects. Here's a partial list of what you probably know about customers across your enterprise:

- Original contract date
- Length of time as a customer
- Industry
- Geography
- Contacts
- Contract value
- Contract growth rate
- Number of support calls
- Severity level of each support case
- Number of days each support case was open
- Number of invoices delivered
- Number of invoices paid
- Number of invoices overdue when paid
- Average time to pay invoices
- Customer Sat scores and trends
- Customer health score and trends
- If you are a subscription SaaS company:
    - Renewal date
    - Every single click ever made in your product

And that list could go on much longer. But the point is made. There is a lot of data about your customers, which allows you deep intelligence into when to contact them and with what message. That kind of touch can be done at scale via e-mail.

Let's take a look at a specific scenario. Let's say you are a SaaS company, and you released a new reporting feature a couple of months ago that many of your customers have been waiting eagerly for, some for more than six months. Because it's a feature that makes your product much stickier, it's in your best interest to make sure all customers are using it. With the help of the right technology, you can now identify the power user and administrator at every customer who has not yet touched this new feature and send them the following e-mail:

Dear Joe,

Thanks again for being such a loyal customer since July 2012. We are pleased that you are part of our extended family. We've noticed that you responded to our last NPS survey and scored our reporting functionality only 6 out of 10. Thanks again for that response and feedback, and I'm happy to let you know that we've recently shipped a significant enhancement to our reporting, which it looks like you have not yet explored, that allows you to easily combine X and Y into one simple report and very simply create a new dashboard with that information, too. So far, our customers who have used it have given it rave reviews. Acme Manufacturing had <u>this</u> to say about it. In case you missed it, you can find the on-demand training videos for enabling and using this feature <u>here</u> and <u>here</u>. Please check them out and provide feedback through the form that pops up at the end of the second video. We'll enter you into our customer challenge for a chance to win free tickets to next year's summit, when you complete the second video.

Happy reporting! I think you'll find this feature especially useful.

Regards,

Your Customer Success Team

Now tell me that kind of e-mail wouldn't be extremely powerful in your attempts to drive value to your customers. And the same e-mail, with personalized content, could be sent to 20 or 1,000 different customers at the same time and at the same cost—$0. Even if you operate in a low-touch customer success model in which you can afford some one-to-one touches, this might save you 15 phone calls and 30-minute discussions with your customers. If you are in a pure tech-touch model, then there's a good chance your customers have gotten very few touches at all over the years, and this is a chance to truly blow them away with value. If you are a mature B2C company or volume B2B company, there's a good chance you are already doing some kind of targeted loyalty campaigns. It might be disguised as customer marketing or it's part of the user experience in your product: recommendation engines are just another form of customer success. In any case, the need for building loyalty with existing customers has become apparent and may be addressed in some way but is likely not as well defined or executed as you need it to be. It's definitely the customer's world today, and we're just living in it. Customer success is simply the acknowledgment and embracing of that reality. If you haven't already, it might be time to bring those ideas together in one organization or at least a common initiative. One trend in maturing SaaS companies today is that customer marketing is moving closer and closer to customer success, if not under that umbrella already.

Clearly, the tech-touch customer success model is highly applicable to almost any business. Even if you are strictly high touch, there are still some tasks CSMs do that could be automated, giving them more time for strategic activities. Most important, the tech-touch model allows any business to start delivering customer success almost immediately, even if you don't have CSMs or don't call it customer success. The example we just used was built around e-mail, but the earlier example I used from United Airlines involved text messaging, which is potentially even more effective if used properly. Digitized voice messages could also be delivered at scale if that channel might occasionally delight your customers.

The bottom line is simply that customer success can be delivered at scale in an effective and highly relevant way for your customers. Technology has made it possible, and more and more companies are starting to take advantage of that capability.

I hope we've established now that customer success is highly relevant no matter what kind of business you are running. Whether you are B2B SaaS, B2C SaaS, not SaaS but subscription based, not subscription based yet but moving in that direction, or pay-as-you-go, you have a direct need for customer success. This is true whether you have 10 $50 million customers or 50 million $10 customers. In some way, you are probably already doing customer success although you may be referring to it as customer experience, account management, or customer marketing. The name of the organization is really irrelevant. It's the mission and the goal that are important. And if the goal is to drive retention or increase the dollar value of your existing customers, viewing them through the lens of customer success is becoming fundamentally important, and, as with any new idea that is changing business, technology is rushing in to assist in the process.

PART

II

The Ten Laws of Customer Success

4

The Practice of Customer Success

In Part I of this book, we laid the foundation for customer success. We discussed the history of the subscription economy and SaaS and how the concept of customer success was the inevitable result of this new model. We talked about organizing around the philosophy of customer success, and then we got pragmatic about the actual organization called customer success (or something like it) and how it's changing the enterprise by impacting virtually all of the other key organizations, too. And then we debunked the theory that customer success might be relevant only for B2B SaaS companies. The truth is that it's conceptually relevant for every company and can be put into actual practice by not only B2B SaaS companies but also any subscription-based or pay-as-you-go company, including B2C and, more and more, traditional companies that are embracing the promised benefits of becoming customer success–centric and most likely trying to move at least part of their business to subscription.

Now it's time to get very practical. In 2010, Bessemer Venture Partners, a venture capital firm, put together a practical guide for people starting, running, or interested in understanding a SaaS company. It was called *The Ten*

Laws of Cloud Computing also often referred to as the Ten Laws of SaaS. It was extremely well received and has been read by thousands of CEOs and entrepreneurs who wanted to venture into the wonderful world of SaaS. It became the handbook for that time and space and remains a reference guide to this day. In 2015, Bessemer decided to double-down on that success and commission the creation of *The Ten Laws of Customer Success* to provide similar guidance for those wanting to understand and deploy customer success. This section of the book uses that wisdom, authored by 10 different experts, in its entirety with extended commentary from this author.

The Ten Laws of Customer Success is not a practical guide regarding how to do customer success per se. It comes from a slightly higher angle, offering the principles that a *company* striving to be world class as a recurring revenue business will need to embrace and execute at a very high level. Some of the *laws* are mostly applicable to B2B SaaS, while many can be more broadly applied to all the types of companies we described in Chapter 3. We've indicated at the beginning of each of the chapters (one for each law) the relevance of that law to each of the different types of companies we've previously discussed:

- B2B SaaS
- Subscription-based
- Pay-as-you-go
- B2C
- Traditional

This will allow you to skim quickly when it's less relevant and to slow down and absorb what is specifically applicable to your world.

The authors of the Ten Laws were hand-picked for their expertise in customer success across a wide range of businesses including

- SaaS—both B2B and B2C
- On-premise traditional software
- Finance
- Education and training
- Collaboration
- Project management
- Sales enablement
- Customer success management
- Compensation management

I'd like to personally thank each of them for their contributions to the industry and practice of customer success, which goes far beyond this book, and for their specific contributions herein.

One last reminder: *The Ten Laws of Customer Success* answers the question, What does my company need to do to be great at customer success and build a thriving recurring revenue business? Without further ado, here are the 10 laws.

5 | Law 1: Sell to the Right Customer

Author: Ted Purcell, Senior Vice President of Sales and Customer Success, Clarizen

Relevance

	LOW	MEDIUM	HIGH
B2B SaaS	★	★	★
SUBSCRIPTION	★	★	★
PAY-AS-YOU-GO	★	★	★
B2C	★	★	
TRADITIONAL	★	★	★

Executive Summary

Selling to the right customer and being completely aligned with your product market fit (PMF) is a mission that growth companies need to focus on throughout the entire organization. The excitement of closing net new deals, especially ones involving common and well-known brands, is exciting for everyone. This is especially true if they are within your PMF, because then the revenue machine is empowered and your specialized handoff from pre-sales to post-sales can be templatized and scaled to help ensure expansion and reduce churn.

But if your customer isn't the right customer, the impact on your organization can be disastrous. The wrong customers can inhibit your organization and take you away from efforts that drive success, efficiency, and scale. On the other hand, this may be a fine line because these customers can also become critical design partners to help you extend your use case and PMF. The critical point? Be aligned on the aspects of what the right customer for your company is and is not!

The customer is the north star of a company—and its most valuable asset. For a company to live up to its aspirations and expectations at scale, the CSM needs to be the host responsible for the complete customer journey, both inside and outside the company—the ultimate trusted adviser. The end result may be increased expansion and decreased churn, but that is icing on the cake compared to the details that enable that goal.

Revenue doesn't just speak, it shouts. That said, your PMF screams! Your PMF must drive your complete corporate alignment, from product development to operations and throughout the go-to-market funnel. As you grow, customers may begin to surface use cases that ideally build on the foundation of your PMF. If not, they may drive your organization into chaos. An organizational commitment to understanding the data that surfaces during your customer engagement life cycle and to ask whether this is the right customer for you is extremely important. The right customers hone your company's vision, your content, and your onboarding of employees, partners, and customers. And they help optimize your corporate direction. The wrong customers, even those who may come with great brands, the promise of large up-front or potential revenue, or referenceability, may take your valuable resources, mindshare, and company down a very dangerous rat hole.

To maximize effectiveness as a SaaS growth company, you will be confronted with this question—Is this customer the right one for us?

In your efforts to optimize a SaaS revenue machine, alignment at all levels and aspects of the company drives focus, specialization, and the ability to effectively scale. Although the product teams must focus on delivering to the PMF, they still need to be aware of and responsive to customer needs and the reality of the market as it evolves. If this alignment is not strong, it can erode a company's focus and ability to execute and scale—to enable and ultimately deliver for the right customers as they start showing up at high volumes and velocity. The right customers may help mature and calibrate a company's PMF and innovation agenda. The wrong customer, who is not aligned with your target market and core PMF, may put constraints on every aspect of your company's go-to-market motion. The key is building a communication mechanism and a process to surface risks early on. Presales, sales, and scoping within the services/statement of work (SOW) build phase are critical points in the feedback loop to mutually surface risks and ultimately change customer direction or put a stop to the sales process with a particular prospect. For this to be effective, your sales team must have a clear and complete picture of the customer context beyond simple product features and functionality. Your sales team must understand the perceived business value and who, how, and why it will affect and influence customers.

Marketing, sales, and customer success, fully aligned with the product, provide a strong enabler of the myriad requests and demands that come from an evolving and maturing customer base. It is incumbent on sales and customer success teams to manage growth and drive scale in concert with the feedback loop from the customer base to maintain alignment with your target market and PMF. This requires strong leadership and a commitment to understanding that the right customers will enable us to be more responsive to the target market and help focus resources on the right efforts, making not only your customers but also your own employees more successful.

How Do You Define the Right Customer?

Does it encompass a particular use case or line of business, a particular industry vertical, or a particular size of customer that fits with your existing product? Is it based on analyzing your current customer base and what's working today or analyzing the size of various addressable markets where you are not currently playing and deciding which ones to target and, potentially, which customers to deprioritize or completely abandon? In the end, it includes a bit of all these factors, but the CEO must be aligned with and committed to the PMF, including the right target customer profile.

Once you have defined the profile of the ideal customer or ideal customer segment, your operational go-to-market engine needs to align with that profile. Operationally, it all starts with selling to the right customer, which means starting at the very top of your revenue funnel. Marketing must target the right kinds of customers, and sales must quickly disqualify those who aren't a great fit, going beyond typical methodology and key qualification steps such as budget, time frame, and executive sponsorship.

The churn itself is only the tip of the iceberg; the cost of signing customers that you can't make successful could be enormous. First, you incur the customer acquisition cost (CAC) of bringing these customers onboard. But the biggest cost is the opportunity cost of applying resources to the wrong customers and, inevitably, doubling down on those customers when they struggle. These resources could have gone to helping other customers who have a greater opportunity for higher customer LTV.

Your message and your brand are empowered by the right content, which needs to be put in the right context in front of the right people at the right time. The customer profile must be assessed at every stage of the funnel, with a commitment to providing a consultative and trusted adviser approach to your customer interactions—even when it is to prevent customers from going down a path that creates complexity, cost, and ultimate derailment. This approach requires investment, including continual messaging to your teams to establish and reaffirm this commitment.

There may be instances when the right target customers are not met with the right internal customer alignment, therefore putting them at potential risk of becoming the wrong customers. Sales and customer support hygiene is critical here. Surprisingly, some customers have become our storybook customers even though they were not the right customer profile initially. Establish executive sponsorship and reach higher and wider in an organization not only to position your product in the right context but also to showcase your customer success–oriented culture to drive a successful customer engagement life cycle. This will help you establish the right cadence with the customer as well as preserving your *trusted adviser* brand, ultimately helping you ascertain whether solving for the internal customer context will drive you to the right customer profile.

When a company is in scale mode, the communication and message of the *right customer commitment* must be consistent and continually reaffirmed. This alignment will drive the top of the funnel activity through your marketing and demand-generation efforts: to sales, to onboarding/professional services, to customer success, and back to product again, building on your referenceability and ultimately leading to reduced churn and improved expansion results.

Sales and customer hygiene are also important, and the process enables the data, which leads to decision making that drives the right results. In an ideal world, a company would sell only to its ideal customer, but we know that growth companies face tremendous pressure to drive revenue growth. As such, it may be necessary to expand the definition of the ideal customer to optimize growth. In that case, it's important to also have a scalable mechanism in place to capture the customer profile so you're able to track and assess the ideal customers, including important metrics such as resource allocation, CAC ratio, net churn, and customer LTV. Various SaaS tools such as Salesforce, Marketo, Gainsight, and Clarizen have the ability to leverage the open application programming interface (API) architecture of these systems to connect them for seamless data flow, so it's possible to capture customer-fit criteria early in the go-to-market cycle and track these data throughout the revenue funnel.

You may also choose to define unique processes for less-than-ideal customer segments. For example, you may choose different business requirements, such as requiring a certain profile of customers to purchase a specific services package. You may choose to invest in a higher-touch process during key risk points, such as deeper CSM engagement during the adoption phase to work to neutralize risk early and to get the customer on the right track. Alternatively, you might choose to minimize investment through lower-touch and one-to-many approaches, such as webinars and self-help, web-based resources to focus limited resources on higher-LTV customers.

Prioritize a scalable system to capture churn reasons and to analyze these data on a regular basis, with product and customer teams to slice and dice the data across various customer segments. Understand what percent of churns were driven by poor adoption, what percent were driven by product fit issues or product gaps versus customer needs, and what percent were driven by factors that were hard to affect, such as merger, acquisition, restructuring, and bankruptcy.

It's also important to analyze your incentive processes across the company and determine how to align them to reinforce the need to focus on the right customer segments. Clearly, your customer success leadership is incented to reduce churn and partner with sales to accelerate expansions. Are your sales leaders incented to reduce churn, thus incenting them to not sell to the wrong customers? How about your product leadership and an incentive on customer retention? If we've established the point that customer LTV and minimizing churn are some of the critical key performance indicators (KPIs) for any SaaS company's success and valuation, doesn't it make sense for all functional leaders to share those variables in their incentives?

Another factor to consider is organizational structure and how it does or does not align to focus the organization on selling to the right customers. Do your sales and customer success organizations report to a chief revenue officer who holds a holistic view of both new business and retained business to help drive the right decisions about which customers to target and which ones to walk away from? If sales and customer success are independent silos, do you provide your customer success leadership veto power over deals that are not a fit?

The feedback from sales and customer success is tremendously important for any high-growth SaaS company to evolve your product and strengthen your PMF. It's critical if you choose to broaden your lens to nonideal customers or to adjacent customer segments beyond your core market. It's also key to capture customer segment information for new feature requests. Without that designation, your product team may incorrectly assess and prioritize where they dedicate product development resources. It's also important to define processes and data flows that scale as the business grows, and it becomes harder and harder to align on priorities because of communication challenges.

Of course, your agenda and your strategy may evolve and mature as you scale, as will your target-customer profile, to set the example for the organization and the company. Referenceability is everything to a company, and building the right content in a value-oriented context should drive the right behavior—not only to acquire more customers but also to set the agenda for your own people, especially as you hire and bring on new employees.

The right customer journey, in combination with the right PMF, with top-down alignment on the priorities of the organization, driven by a collaborative and transparent agenda for your employees, partners, and customers, will help minimize noise and drive operational excellence throughout your customer engagement life cycle. Moreover, it will ultimately help you focus on selling to the right customer.

Additional Commentary

Dave Kellogg, CEO at Host Analytics, recently said this to me: "Ninety percent of all churn happens at the time of sale." In other words, at least in his business, almost all churn happens because they've sold to the wrong customer. This is probably true to varying degrees across all businesses. And the actual *cost* of selling to the wrong customer is enormous. The wrong customer is always harder to onboard, taxing your team's time and abilities. This often leads to greater demands on your product team as well. The burden then gets passed on to the customer success and support teams when the onboarding project is complete, and the struggle exacerbates when your customer success team has to scramble to configure and execute an outside-the-box use case on behalf of the customer and then train the customer on how to use it. Then, the bell rings 90 days pre-renewal and, with the customer at risk, a SWAT team is assembled to "save" the customer, often including an executive or two. In this situation, the renewal is secured about 50 percent of the time and usually only by dropping the price, refunding some money, or extending the customer some free months due to their challenges. All this does is kick the can down the road with the same difficulties still unresolved in the new contract term. For the 50 percent of customers who do churn at this point, the lost dollars are painful. But the opportunity cost of all the hours and effort poured into the customer only to have them fail hurts much more. Think of that time and energy being channeled instead into good customers with the opportunity to grow and thrive. The last negative might be the biggest one—the word-of-mouth that will go forth from this failed customer. Although much of the blame might actually fall on him, that's not likely to be the story when that customer talks to friends and colleagues about you.

High Touch

High-touch businesses are especially affected by not selling to the right customer. By definition, high-touch customers are your most valuable, and that means they are most likely the highest-paying ones, too. However, there are more than dollars on the line. Also, every other part of the post-sales world is staffed to provide these customers a better experience and a higher likelihood of success. This means that a 10 percent or 20 percent increase in the burden of onboarding, training, support, and customer success is 10 percent or 20 percent of a much larger number than in your low-touch or tech-touch world. The brand value and brand recognition of these customers is almost always much higher, too, so the cost of their negative advocacy is more painful than from a lesser-known customer.

Low Touch

The pain of losing a low-touch customer is not as great as a high-touch customer. However, there are more customers of the low-touch variety, so if you are not diligent about selling to the right customer, you may find yourself with a significant burden here. And, because they are low touch, your ability to manage the resulting crises adequately or to find the resources to save the customer are slim. This can be just as costly as with your high-touch tier. It may be even more costly in one way. Because there are more of these kinds of customers, they will, in aggregate, know more people, so the negative word-of-mouth might even be greater than for high touch, even if the brand value of each individual customer is lower.

Tech Touch

Now take the problems defined previously for high touch, multiply that by 10 (or more) for low touch because of the volume, and multiply that again by 10 for tech touch. Each tier downward gives you significantly less chance to save an individual customer. Think of the impossibility of saving a customer who is not really a good fit for your product, simply by sending them e-mails or getting them to attend webinars. Highly unlikely to bear fruit, right?

So, how do you mitigate the chances of selling to the wrong customer since it's so important to not do that?

- Use data, not just anecdotes. If you are going to be rigorous in who you sell to, it needs to be data driven. You can't just say, "I think we sold before to a customer like that, and it didn't work out." It needs to be more along these lines: "We've done deals with 31 customers who match the same industry, discount, use cases, and price-point profile of this one, and 14 of them churned at the time of first renewal and another four at their second renewal. Eight of them have not had a renewal come up yet. The remaining five renewed but at an average contract decline of 14 percent. In addition, our average NPS score across the remaining 13 customers is 5.2, and their average health score is 38.7."

- Give your vice president of customer success veto power over deals in the pipeline. This is bold and a little dangerous, but it can work. It's a little bit like giving your customer support team veto power over whether a release should go out. You can make the argument that they should have that power because they'll have to live with the result of the decision. If retention is truly a key focus of your company, then the person who owns retention needs to wield a lot of authority.

- Put your customer success team under your sales VP. We don't recommend this as we discussed in Chapter 3. But, if it's a major problem that sales continues to sell to the wrong customer, making the same VP who makes the selling decision have to suffer the consequences of those decisions will definitely change their focus. That's why we had a sales leader who also owns customer success write this particular law. If you don't put customer success under sales, and, to a lesser degree, even if you do, your CEO will need to be deeply involved in balancing the need to sell more new customers with the need for a high retention rate.

- Make sure your VP of sales (and all executives) is incented on retention, not just new business. You could take this argument all the way down to the individual sales reps, but they don't typically worry about a year or more down the road so that may not have the impact you are looking for. But, if your sales leader, who is probably also compensated on overall company performance, is incented on retention just as he is on new business, you'll find this will definitely have an impact.

- Read Law 10 carefully. Customer success has to be a top-down commitment, which means the CEO needs to drive the company with long-term, retention thinking, not just grabbing deals to make quarterly numbers. Most likely it will end up being his call to say "no" to deals and certainly to properly incent and enforce the right company behavior. He and the board are incented above all else on long-term company success.

6 | Law 2: The Natural Tendency for Customers and Vendors Is to Drift Apart

Author: Karen Pisha, Senior Vice President of Customer Success, Code42

Relevance

	LOW	MEDIUM	HIGH
B2B SaaS	★	★	★
SUBSCRIPTION	★	★	★
PAY-AS-YOU-GO	★	★	★
B2C	★	★	★
TRADITIONAL	★	★	★

Executive Summary

Customers and vendors start off their relationship like two boats side by side in the middle of a lake. But if both boats are unoccupied, they will soon begin to drift apart. Over a longer period of time, it's highly likely that the two boats will end up very far apart. What would change that natural tendency? Simple. Put someone in one of the boats with a pair of oars. Better yet, put someone in each boat with oars.

Change is the enemy here. If nothing changed, customers and vendors might very well stay tight. But change is the constant. People change in both companies. Business models change. Products change. Leadership and direction change. And on it goes. Only willful, proactive interaction on the part of one or both companies will overcome the natural drift caused by constant change. This is why customer success organizations have come into existence. Customer success organizations and practices intervene to push the customer and the vendor back together. They get into one of the boats and start rowing.

The long-term health of your business is directly tied to your ability to retain customers and prevent churn. No other metric is responsible for more meetings or more sleepless nights. In a recurring revenue business, most of your revenue comes after the initial sale. In fact, in many SaaS companies, the expected lifetime value of a customer is 10 times the value of the initial sale. As a limiting factor to growth, churn negatively affects both growth and company valuation. It also has a terrible impact on morale. Everyone hates to lose a customer, but, in a recurring revenue business, the costs are acute. The biggest cost, as mentioned in the previous chapter, may not even be the value of the customer's contract, but the resources that were burned acquiring, onboarding, assisting, and often trying to save a customer who eventually churns. Churn increases with the size of your customer base, which makes it incredibly difficult to overcome.

Churn can be defined as the percentage of subscribers to a service that discontinue their subscription to that service in a given time period. Because all companies invest significant resources acquiring their customers, it's critical to be sure customers stick around as long as possible to generate the largest possible return on the initial investment. The longer your customers stay, the larger the return.

In a recurring revenue business the concept of *partial churn* is also valuable to understand. That is simply the loss of contract dollars in a situation in which the customer does not leave you. Partial churn can come from a product churning, unused licenses being returned, or customers negotiating a deeper discount because of challenges they encountered working with you or a perception of receiving lower value than they originally expected.

So why do customers decide to part ways with their established vendors in search of greener pastures? What triggers customers to leave the nest? Does churn result from predictable patterns or a series of unpredictable, random occurrences? Many hours have been spent analyzing this problem, and research and anecdotal experience tells us it's not random.

It might sound obvious, but if you want to stop your customers from looking at your competitors, you need to make them successful using your product or service. It's not as easy as it sounds. The definition of successful customers varies widely and depends on many factors. Most companies believe that successful customers are a direct result of product adoption, engagement, and product usage. It's also critical to make sure they are getting the business benefits they set out to achieve when they selected you as their vendor of choice. One thing to consider is that sometimes the most successful customers appear to be unhappy. This tends to happen when customers are pushing the boundaries of your product or your organization. Do not mistake demanding for unsuccessful. Oftentimes, the opposite is true. The traits that make a customer demanding are also likely to ensure that they are getting maximum value from your product and are simply asking for more.

While there are many reasons why customers cancel, most companies don't catch on until it's too late to save the account. This is especially critical for subscription-based companies. Here are some of the top reasons why customers churn. The real trick is putting measures in place to look for the warning signs and acting on the data when you see the signals.

Financial Return or Business Value Not Realized

It's possible that the initial business case wasn't founded on accurate data, or maybe the circumstances changed internally. In either event, lack of ROI creates a big risk for you.

- **Telltale signs:** Decrease in usage or inactivity after signup.
- **Steps you can take:** Leverage the customer success team, if you have one, to review the client's goals and guide clients through the product adoption phases so they get value early. Continuously look for ways

to expand use of your product so it supports more functions, thereby generating more business value (i.e., higher return). If your world is purely tech touch, then you need to find creative ways to reinforce your value proposition, why the customer purchased in the first place, and how to take advantage of the resources available to get more value out of the product and your associated services.

Stalled or Prolonged Implementation

Customers are usually antsy to get started, but all too often, they lose their momentum or focus after the project starts. If customers can't get their products into production, they aren't seeing any value.

- **Telltale signs:** Customer fails to get the product in an operational production mode.
- **Steps you can take:** Define packages and services offerings that provide quicker time to value by getting customers started on the customer journey. This may include defining smaller phases that get the customer using your product for a subset of their overall scope.

Loss of Project Sponsor or Power User

The transition of a project sponsor or power user creates a risk for your long-term success. In some cases, all the background information about why your product was purchased and the keys to managing the application reside in one or two key people.

- **Telltale signs:** The customer goes dark. You can't reach the project owner or sponsor.
- **Steps you can take:** Offer training for new users to make sure that more than one person in the organization knows how to use your product. Strive to maintain or create high-level relationships to keep management on board and to fall back on when one of your key champions leaves or takes on a new role.

Low Rate of Product Adoption

Customers who are not using your product to support their business requirements are likely to find another option or go back to their old method of doing business.

- **Telltale signs:** Customers aren't using your product at all, or you have seen a decline in usage.
- **Steps you can take:** Develop programs to work with customers to assess their business needs, and guide them through a customer journey that outlines the functionality they can use in the product. Ensuring that more users are logging into the product and supporting a broader set of functions makes your product more sticky (and harder to replace). Also, building a library of customer ROI stories and testimonials for use when interest or momentum seems to wane can be really beneficial.

Acquisition by a Company That Uses Another Solution

Company acquisitions account for some degree of churn in most recurring revenue or pay-as-you-go companies.

- **Telltale signs**: Your customer contact tells you that the organization is being acquired or that the new company leadership is forcing another solution.
- **Steps you can take:** This is a tough one. In some cases, you may have the opportunity to present the value of your product or service to the new company leadership. This may give you a chance to maintain (or grow) your footprint. In many cases, however, the die has been cast and your product is not on the approved list, thereby creating uncontrollable churn.

Lack of Product Features

Competition is heating up for every product and company. The draw of new features, such as more intuitive UIs or mobile or social capabilities, plus the lure of lower prices, are driving many companies to switch vendors.

- **Telltale signs:** Your customer is asking for new features, more product enhancements, or more aggressive pricing.
- **Steps you can take:** Make sure your CSM is up to speed on your product road map and understands where you are making investments in the product. If you don't have a customer success team, find another way to communicate the positive future vision for your product and company to existing customers. Get customer feedback about product

direction and ask customers what they think. Share feedback with your product management team to let them know what matters most to customers. Engaging customers and making them feel like they are part of your process can be a very powerful initiative.

New Leadership Driving Shift in Direction or Strategy

New customer leadership can drive a shift in direction or strategy. Sometimes leaders bring strong opinions or biases about the product they used in the past, and they force an evaluation or replacement of your product.

- **Telltale signs:** You are being asked to participate in a request for proposal (RFP) or solution evaluation process.
- **Steps you can take:** With the support of your project owner or sponsor, place a proactive call to the new leader. Offer to provide an overview of your organization, product, and value proposition. Reinforce value received and opportunities to get additional ROI from extended capabilities and usage. It's important to get ahead of this at all costs because the comparison of your existing installed product, with all its warts, does not usually stand up well against PowerPoint slides and demos from your competition.

Customer Affected by Poor Product Quality or Performance Issues

Product or performance issues can create significant pain for your customers and put them in a position in which they are looking for a better, more stable solution.

- **Telltale signs:** Your customer has logged an increased volume of support tickets or escalated cases.
- **Steps you can take:** First off, find a way to track early warning signs so you can get ahead of this before it becomes a crisis. An alert when a customer goes over a certain threshold of support tickets, maybe three in any given week, sets off an action plan, such as a phone call or an e-mail campaign. If you are in a high-touch or low-touch situation, you need to be knowledgeable and empathetic, offering solutions and alternatives in a timely fashion. Escalate internally and let your customers know that their issues are receiving the highest level of attention. Stay

on top of issues and proactively provide updates on progress. Customers understand that software isn't perfect and they value the relationship and support they receive to get to resolution. Unfortunately, if the issues persist or create significant impact, you are at risk of losing your customer.

Your Product Is Not the Right Solution

Creative salespeople can find ways to sell products even when they're not the perfect fit for your customer's requirements. See the previous chapter and Law 1 for more insights here. In some cases, customers will buy your product to solve a need that doesn't match your sweet spot.

- **Telltale signs:** Your customer's understanding of your core product capabilities is not accurate or the customer is asking for features that are outside your wheelhouse.
- **Steps you can take:** Educate the sales team on the use cases and customer parameters that create the ideal customer experience. Partner during the sales process to help identify where prospects do not fit the ideal customer profile and offer alternatives to the way the customer is solving the business requirement. Teach the professional services team the warning signs and how to identify risks early in the project. Reread the previous chapter for more ways to avoid selling to the wrong customer.

The Human Factor

Even the best customer success professionals will occasionally not mesh with your customers. It's important to pay close attention to all the customer-facing people on your team and watch for the warning signs when the matchup might not be ideal.

- **Telltale signs:** You may receive less-than-glowing feedback from a customer on a call or in a survey about your team member. You may also get the feedback secondhand, through partners or individuals who are connected to your customer.
- **Steps you can take:** Don't ignore negative feedback. Proactively reach out to your customers and seek their input and opinion about your

team member. You need to quickly determine whether the relationship can be fixed or whether you need to replace it. Delaying the need to replace a resource can bring long-term negative effects.

The bottom line is that you must put proactive procedures in place to monitor the health of your customers. The more you understand your customers, their business needs, and the ways they are using your product, the better off you will be when it comes time for them to renew their contract or decide whether you continue to be their vendor of choice. Whenever possible, proactive outreach from your customer success management team, or intervention through your tech-touch channels such as e-mail, webinars, or community, can make a big difference in your long-term relationships and overall customer health. A few great ways to maintain contact include:

- Proactive outreach from the CSM or an executive
- Timely, relevant e-mail content
- High-quality customer webinars that provide ideas about how to extend use of the product
- Updates and involvement from a robust customer community
- Regular user group meetings
- Customer advisory boards
- User conferences

Additional Commentary

Change really is your enemy. It's very hard to maintain the level of value, or perception of value, that you had originally with even your best customers. This is true in consumer applications, too. For most people, Facebook's value was highest in the first few months that they used it. It's not that the value went away. In fact, the potential value of the product has almost certainly increased as more and more effort is put into it and features come out of it. But the end user's perception of value often goes down as the novelty wears off or the value begins to be taken for granted or your competition erodes the differentiation that your customers see in your product versus theirs. The battle to retain and increase the value of your existing customers is never-ending. Your only choice is to deal with it.

High Touch

If you have high-touch customers, this challenge is both easier and harder. It can be easier because of the tight relationship you have with them and the level of engagement they likely have with you as a company, including helping define your product road map as well as being very demanding about all aspects of your existing product. It's also easier because the relationship does not change as much as with the other models once the sale is complete. In some ways, the intensity of the relationship may even go up after the deal is done because the potential LTV of these customers tends to be much higher than the initial deal, and, as a result, we tend to throw more bodies at them.

On the other hand, the challenge can be harder with your high-touch clients if only because the stakes are so much higher. But it's also more difficult to maintain executive relationships at the right level to help you navigate the changes that are happening on your customer's end. The power and authority that your champion has today can change overnight with reorganizations and new leadership. Organizations tend to be much more complex and politics much more prevalent at larger companies. All of this works against your ability to align, and stay aligned, with the right people who will continue to support and vouch for your product.

Low Touch

The challenges for low-touch customers are not surprising. They are much more likely to go through dramatic company-wide changes than your bigger customers. And, because you don't talk to them as frequently, it's more difficult to comprehend the magnitude of these changes and how they will affect you. If you see these customers as individual entities, which of course you need to do at times, you can miss the forest for the trees. In some ways, low-touch and tech-touch customers force you to do things as a vendor that are more positive and far-reaching than your high-touch customers. Because you typically won't overreact to the needs of one or two of these clients, the focus required in order to retain and satisfy them goes to the things that are most scalable—processes and product. Ultimately, your product is by far the most scalable part of your business. Pouring energy and effort relentlessly into making your product, and the supporting processes to deliver, enable, and support it better, will help you grow in a much more efficient way than delivering to the special needs of your largest clients. Embracing this truth can be a very positive cultural attitude.

Another aspect of this truth that is important to understand is that your retention/churn targets for your low-touch tier of customers versus your high-touch customers should be different. With very few exceptions, the retention rate as you go down your pyramid of tiers will be lower. Understanding and accepting that can allow you to not hyperfocus on one or two of these customers at the expense of improving the overall aspects of your business that are more scalable, such as processes and product.

Tech Touch

As will often be the case as we discuss each of the Ten Laws and how they relate to the different touch models, whatever is true for low-touch versus high-touch is exaggerated and accelerated for tech-touch clients. Everything I said about the challenges and positives for your low-touch customers is true in spades for tech-touch customers. Because you never talk to them, except in large groups where real feedback is limited, the likelihood of finding out that their business model or organization is changing is very low. Three things can provide great assistance in this scenario:

1. **Surveys**. This might be the best way of getting consistent feedback from these customers. Asking them to tell you whether their leadership or business model has changed is probably not useful. But getting consistent feedback on the value of various parts of your product can be extremely valuable. If this kind of information can be gathered and communicated to your product team, who should be constantly watching the market and adapting to the aggregate changes that are happening, you should be able to adapt quickly to the changing product requirements.
2. **Community** A thriving community will provide you consistent insight into what customers are thinking and saying. It's also invaluable in posing questions and getting rapid responses from a large group. Make sure you are giving as much as you are taking in your community but make use of the power it provides.

3. **Understanding churn**. In a B2C world, this will also most likely have to be done through surveys. In the B2B world, even for very low end customers, it may be worth the money or time to follow up with a select few churned customers to truly understand what broke down and how it could have been avoided, if at all. In any case, it's often more valuable to understand why a customer churned than to understand why they stayed because the churn is often a more discrete event with considered rationale. Understanding this well *must* be a part of running a recurring revenue business. See Chapter 11 for more on this topic.

High-touch customers may be your lever to financial success, but low-touch and tech-touch customers may provide equally valuable levers with regard to scaling and efficiency.

7 | Law 3: Customers Expect You to Make Them Wildly Successful

Author: Nello Franco, Senior Vice President of Customer Success, Talend

Relevance

	LOW	MEDIUM	HIGH
B2B SaaS	★	★	★
SUBSCRIPTION	★	★	★
PAY-AS-YOU-GO	★	★	★
B2C	★	★	
TRADITIONAL	★	★	

Executive Summary

Customers don't buy your solution to use its features and functions. They buy your solution (and buy into the relationship with you) because they want to achieve a business objective. Just as sales organizations are using a *challenger* sales approach, customer success organizations and practices need to provide new insights and challenges. As Ben Horowitz said in his 2015 commencement address at Columbia University: "There's no value in telling someone what they already know."

The value your customer places on your relationship isn't defined only by your product's features and functions; it's also defined by everything else your company does to help make your customers better at what they do. That includes enablement, content marketing, online resources, and, in the case of relationships with larger enterprises, direct engagement by subject matter experts. In some cases, delivering a message that goes against conventional (and popular) wisdom can be difficult, but in the end, delivering a challenging message that is in your customer's best interest will strengthen your relationship. In a world where retention is critical this is not just an opportunity, it's an obligation. Allowing your customers to go down the wrong path will bring potentially disastrous results, so challenging customers to do it the right way is mandatory.

Delivering wild success requires you to understand three fundamental things:

1. How is your customer measuring success? In other words, what is the customer's unit of measure (time saved, incremental revenue, reduced cost, specific financial impact of increased quality), and what results does the customer need to declare victory?
2. Is the customer achieving that value (or at least on a realistic path to achieving it)?
3. What has the customer's experience been with you along the way?

Wild success doesn't happen by chance. It happens because both you and your customer have a real stake in mutual success. You both share and understand those objectives, you measure and monitor progress against those objectives, you ask hard questions, and you continuously strive to raise the bar when setting new objectives.

The truth is that it takes more than a great product to make your customers successful. In the enterprise, you've won the deal because your sales team has done an outstanding job of selling the benefits of your company, painting a vision, and setting expectations that there will be significant payback with your solution. In a recent customer meeting, a forward-thinking chief information officer (CIO) expressed to me his concern with many software vendors: "None of them challenge us. They come in, install the software, and then move on. I'd like to understand what we're currently doing that we should be doing differently. We're not just paying for a product—we want expertise as well." In a sense, he was telling us: "You sold us on vision and expertise. That's our expectation. Now deliver."

Unless you can start by delivering some value quickly, while executives are still excited, you risk losing momentum and falling into what Gartner has called the *trough of disillusionment* (see Figure 7.1).

With early proof points, your customers' perception of success will be on a much flatter curve (see Figure 7.2).

In addition to ensuring that you're tracking to ultimate success for your customer, set your customers up for a quick win. Define an initial milestone and track that time to first value (shown in Figure 7.2 as "Phase 1 Value"). It may be as simple as delivering an initial proof of concept with basic functionality, but it will quickly provide evidence to your customer (both your immediate sponsor as well as executives or board members) that the decision to go with your technology was a good one. It's also important to prove value quickly, because any expansion plans you may have with the customer will be predicated on your success. Early wins keep that momentum going.

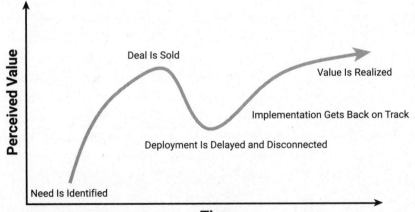

Figure 7.1   Delayed Value Scenario

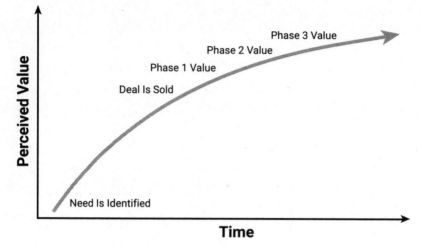

Figure 7.2   Improved Value Scenario

An early win will also be extremely helpful if you encounter any challenges (technical, business, environmental, or political) in future phases. It will allow your sponsor to point to the value already achieved as a way to flatten obstacles and rally support.

Installing on-premise software, provisioning a user account for a SaaS solution, making your B2C solution or mobile app brain-dead easy to use, or even providing basic training on the functionality of your product are simply table stakes. Those activities get you in the game, but they aren't what make you win. If your company innovates—and which successful ones don't?—it's important that you outwardly communicate the benefits of that innovation and, critically, how your customers should use your capabilities to be more effective at what they do. Great companies need to provide this expertise and guidance in a way that scales. It isn't just about having highly skilled professional services consultants who come in on a fee-for-services basis (although that's very important when serving the enterprise, as well as some subset of highly technical solutions). You'll also need great content (knowledge base, best practices, how-tos) and an efficient means for delivering it.

The main reason that your customer bought your product in the first place isn't because your features are cool. It's because your customer has a job to do and expects your solution (and your company) to help them do it better. For example, if your company provides a digital marketing solution, you need to provide the tools, technology, training, and supporting content to make your customers better digital marketers, not just a way for them to send e-mails. More importantly, you need to continuously provide the customer with examples of how they can use your solution to be more effective, how other customers are using it to be more effective, and, if you have the aggregate data, how some of the customer's key metrics (usage or otherwise) compare to similar companies or industry averages. Without a benchmark of comparison or a target to achieve, the customer's current performance data have limited value.

To Help Your Customers Become Wildly Successful, You Must First Understand What Success Means to Them

To manage your customers through the journey of wild success, you always need to know three things about them:

1. **How are they measuring success?** Specifically, what is the key metric, or "unit of currency," that they're using to measure success, and how many units will the customer need to add/save/remove/reduce to claim that they've gotten value from your solution? You should also know how the customers as a team (irrespective of your solution) are being measured for performance.
2. **According to that metric (or metrics), are they achieving success?** Or, if it's a work in progress, is the customer on track to succeed within the expected time frame?
3. **What is their experience along the way?** While the first two questions are pretty clear-cut and quantitative, this one is less so; however, it is incredibly important. It will drive the tone of your relationship and interactions with your customers. Even if your customers achieve their objectives using your technology, if their experience is painful and requires more effort than they believe is necessary, then you've significantly increased their cost (both tangible and intangible) of achieving success and their chances of churning.

Return on Investment Isn't a Concept; It's an Equation

Another area that receives intense focus during the sales cycle but may fall through the cracks after implementation is the quantification of ROI. If you're a provider of customer success solutions, your customers might have the following objectives:

- Reduce churn
- Find upsell opportunities
- Improve the ability to scale their team

While it is difficult to attribute the degree to which your solution is helping the customer achieve each of the three preceding objectives, the first thing to do, if possible, is to quantify the expected results. For example, reduce churn by how much? Identify how many new upsell opportunities, and of what size? How much total value? How much productivity gain do you expect to see in your team? How do you measure productivity? Is there a way that you can tie use of the product (or particular features of the product) to team scalability? Can you identify a few key metrics associating health scores for a certain percentage of customers in a certain tier as a point of first value? After you understand the expectations, set them as a clear target.

Get on a Cadence and Track Your Progress

Use regular business reviews (with your higher-touch customers) as a way to track progress toward the objectives and targets you've jointly defined. If your customers understand that you have a vested stake in their success and you share a common objective with them, they'll be willing to engage with you on a regular basis to collaborate on how they can get there. Regular strategic business reviews (SBRs), quarterly or otherwise, focusing on these objectives, give you and your customers a *reason* to engage on a regular basis. These objectives also help frame the conversation for a business review. I've seen too many quarterly business reviews (QBRs) poorly attended because they weren't working toward clearly stated and understood success criteria. Product roadmap updates and a review of open support cases will carry a QBR only so far. In fact, a QBR that covers only those topics is extremely defensive. There's no way for you or your customer to win if all you're talking about are features that don't yet exist and features that aren't working properly.

A business review must be part of a broader context of a journey to well understood success. If you have a clear understanding of the customer's success criteria, then at the end of each QBR, you should be setting measurable objectives for the next one. I met with a customer recently who has an objective to migrate billions of rows of data to a new repository within the next two months using our product. While our CSM is going to have a number of conversations in the interim to ensure that the customer achieves that goal, the larger team is certainly going to review progress against that quantifiable objective in the next QBR.

Success Isn't a Destination; It's a Journey

Although your customers may have set out initial success criteria, part of the value you bring as a partner is helping customers define what they should think about next. You know and understand the value your product can potentially bring to your customers. You also know how other customers are using your product successfully. This is a perfect opportunity for you to give your customers guidance about what they should be thinking about next. If they just used your customer success automation product to increase their retention rates from 85 percent to 88 percent, you now have an opportunity to show them how best-in-class companies are achieving 90 percent or more renewal rates—and how your partnership can help them get there. For lower-touch customers, you can achieve this objective through content marketing and communication of online best practices. For higher-touch customers, this can (and should) be an opportunity for executive alignment. It's an opportunity to influence each other's strategy, as well as an opportunity to strengthen the relationship. A good tool to use to help drive customer direction beyond first value is an effectiveness model—demonstrating value and progress (http://blog.nellofranco.com/2013/07/09/demonstrating-value-and-progress-to-your-customers/)—that you can use to set objectives and timelines to help your customers better achieve their business objectives via your partnership.

In Theory, There's No Difference between Theory and Reality—but in Reality, There Is

All this sounds great in theory. However, unless you have perfect alignment and agreement on everything throughout your customer relationship (starting with the sales process), you're going to have cases in which customers won't come to the table, won't provide you with key data, will be challenging and confrontational, and may have a different understanding and set of expectations than you do—possibly thanks to an overly optimistic sales effort. You may run into challenges with your product. Your support or services organization may not always deliver impeccable service. All I can say is: welcome to customer success. These are all challenges that you have to deal with, and you must have difficult conversations as soon as possible when issues arise. Issues won't go away by themselves. Customers, however, will.

Approached properly, these conversations are, at minimum, incredible learning experiences. The best perspective for your company to take is to look at itself through the lens of your customer. No matter how hard you try to imagine how your customers feel about something or what they think, you won't know until they tell you. Candid customer conversations are a valuable source of information—sometimes epiphanies—for your company.

Challenging times are also a great opportunity to cement a relationship. I have heard it said that the strongest steel is forged by the fires of hell. If you've worked through a difficult situation collaboratively with a customer and shown your true colors as a partner or if you've accepted responsibility, identified short-term milestones—then met those milestones—regained trust, and made your customer successful, then you'll understand and empathize with this statement. If customers aren't following through on their side of a commitment, then you'll need to escalate, strategize with your sales team or other business functions, and figure out how to have the necessary difficult conversation with the right person or people. Customer success is everyone's responsibility. Use all the resources available to you. Your customer is expecting you to.

It's true that customers expect you to make them wildly successful. It's also true that they're highly motivated to be wildly successful with you. In fact, they're at least as big a stakeholder in your mutual success as you are. Your customers are demanding because they want to be successful. Challenging your customers isn't always an easy task. It requires a relationship, mutual respect, and a sense that you both are working toward the same objective. A customer told me recently at a dinner meeting: "The challenge you posed to us was difficult for us to process and accept. We initially took offense that you, in essence, were telling us that we were wrong, and that caused some tension. Ultimately, however, because we felt that you were in the same boat with us, we accepted it. As a result, it has strengthened our relationship."

Customer feedback about your opportunities for improvement isn't always as obvious as an escalation or a challenge. In most cases, you need to be paying attention to the more subtle clues that there may be risk to your customers' success. Many times, those clues are in what they don't say rather than what they do say. Risk might be indicated by a change in schedule or priorities. In any of these cases, it's critical to get to the root cause of the issue and understand what course corrections you need to make to drive customer success.

Remember, your customers aren't buying a technology. They're buying a solution to a problem, a path to a better way. It's your responsibility to understand the customer's goals and objectives and to steer the customer along that path (in both high-touch and low-touch ways). Once you're able to understand how customers are measuring success, confirm that they're achieving it, and confirm that they're having a positive experience along the way, you'll have the most valuable thing possible: an advocate. And in a world where social media and the network are accelerants that help both negative and positive opinions spread like wildfire, advocacy is priceless.

In combination, the Challenger Sale methodology and the rise of content marketing have created an environment in which customers expect that they have purchased more than just a product to use. They've entered a relationship with a company that is going to make them more effective at achieving their business objectives. As a result, the CSM (as well as the entire customer-facing team) needs to grab the baton and take on the role of challenger throughout the customer life cycle. Wild success doesn't happen by chance. It happens because someone asks hard questions, objectives are measured and monitored, and once those objectives are achieved, someone raises the bar and repeats. Welcome to (wild) customer success.

Additional Commentary

This isn't a knock on millennials, but we do live in an entitlement world. The Internet has truly changed everything but especially expectations. Remember when you used to ponder how many Academy Awards

Anthony Hopkins has won and then never find out the answer? Those days are long gone. Now we have the answer within two minutes of asking the question (or else we're complaining about the Internet Movie Database [IMDb] performance or the lack of Wi-Fi in the restaurant). Technology has also provided us with a plethora of easy-to-use mobile apps like IMDb. All of these things are spoiling our current and future customers with expectations that are very hard to meet. One of those expectations is that the burden is on us (you), not on them, to make them successful. In a subscription-based world, this is a truth whether we like it or not. Because, if we don't do it, one of our competitors will, even if it's bad business policy and too expensive to sustain. We're stuck with this reality, so we need to learn to deal with it. Again, our only option is to embrace it. Fighting it will only waste our energy and passion.

There is a tiny bit of realism left that we can count on, at least temporarily. Everyone accepts that an application that helps you consolidate your financials and close your books every quarter is going to be a bit more complicated and challenging to use than Yelp or Words With Friends. But the gap is definitely narrowing. The most successful business software is definitely borrowing UI tips from consumer apps, and everyone is benefiting from it. But the higher bar is always harder to leap over. Whether we're selling products that require a four-month onboarding process or a product that we download from the App Store and want to use 30 seconds later, the expectation that we will make the lives of our customers much easier every single day is not going to go away.

High Touch

This is the set of customers that seems to most logically fit this particular law. I will argue that the expectations are the same across all tiers *when it comes to competitive differentiation*, not necessarily in comparing Oracle's accounts payable application to your Uber app. For high-touch customers, this burden is very real and falls largely onto the shoulders of individuals. Typically, one person has to understand the customer's definition of success. One person needs to help define ROI and report it to the customer. And one person is responsible for delivering the training required for effective use of the product. These are all things that can be more and more automated over time but, for most products today, belong in the job requirements of an individual.

For a customer success organization, this is definitely where the rubber meets the road. They do not stand alone by any means, and their expectations of help from product, training, onboarding, and support are 100 percent legitimate. But the individual CSM will ultimately bear the burden of ensuring that her customers are wildly successful. As is always the case, customers will participate in that process with varying degrees of ability, direction, and zeal. As we who live in this world know, the success of a customer is often much more up to them than it is up to us. But we bear the responsibility of making it happen regardless because the results if we don't are bad, regardless of blame.

Low Touch

For this particular law, low-touch customers may well be the hardest. The long-term solution is automation to be sure. But the customer's expectation is perfection, as provided by people, if the technology part of the equation isn't meeting their needs. The challenge is obvious—the customer's expectations are that there are people who can help them (which is typically true) if they need it. What customers often fail to understand is that the people resources are not unlimited. It's just a truth we have to deal with that limited resources, in this case people, is a much harder expectation to set and maintain than no resources. Think about the different message we might want to send to these two sets of customers and how that message is heard:

Low touch—"Our process for leading you to success includes all of our technology-based resources. You will have full and unlimited access to our KnowledgeBase, our Best Practices library, and our OnDemand training videos. In addition, your customer success manager/team can be of assistance on a limited basis."

Tech touch—"Our process for leading you to success includes all of our technology-based resources. You will have full and unlimited access to our KnowledgeBase, our Best Practices library, and our OnDemand training videos."

Which of those is less likely to be misunderstood? Which is more likely to be abused? Which is more likely to set the wrong expectations?

Be prepared for the challenges here. They are not insurmountable, but they can be significant.

Tech Touch

The expectations here are pretty easy to set, but don't forget that the bar is really high. Once again, you'll want to find a way to get real feedback from these customers so you can adapt to their needs consistently. You can do this through surveys as we discussed previously. You could also do this within your application. There are many third-party tools available, such as WalkMe, that will guide a user through your app in real time and can help make your customer's journey much more efficient and just plain better. You could also build feedback mechanisms into your app so, for example, you could ask the user whether something is confusing them when they pause for too long on a certain page or a certain step in the process. Don't take lightly the need to handhold your users through your product or process because that's what they expect and that's what your competition is working on.

This is another place where some kind of early warning system can be extremely helpful. If a new customer hasn't reached a certain point of value in your application (as defined by you), a triggered e-mail could be the way to stimulate their progress. This obviously requires mapping out the ideal customer journey and the *must-use* parts of your product so you can intervene in an appropriate and timely fashion.

Generally speaking, the subscription economy puts the customer in charge much more than was previously true. This law speaks to that truth very specifically. If you are going to be great in building a customer success–centric business, you will need to own the burden of making your customers wildly successful.

8 | Law 4: Relentlessly Monitor and Manage Customer Health

Author: Dan Steinman, Chief Customer Officer, Gainsight

Relevance

	LOW	MEDIUM	HIGH
B2B SaaS	★	★	★
SUBSCRIPTION	★	★	★
PAY-AS-YOU-GO	★	★	★
B2C	★	★	★
TRADITIONAL	★	★	★

Executive Summary

Customer health is at the heart of customer success. It not only informs but also drives appropriate action when used properly. It is to customer success what the sales pipeline is to a sales VP—the predictor of future customer behavior. Good customer health equates to a high chance of renewal and upsell. Poor customer health means a lower chance of renewal and upsell. So just as sales VPs manage through their pipeline, customer success teams must manage through customer health.

Given that retention is life or death for a recurring revenue business, monitoring and managing customer health is a core activity for customer success teams: it must be done and done well—and relentlessly.

The title of this law is one of those phrases with which you can play an old word game—read it aloud four times, emphasizing a different word or phrase each time:

- Relentlessly monitor and manage *customer health.*
- Relentlessly monitor and *manage* customer health.
- Relentlessly *monitor* and manage customer health.
- *Relentlessly* monitor and manage customer health.

Each and every idea in this phrase is equally valuable if you are to execute on an aggressive customer success vision. Let's set the stage first and then come back to analyze each piece independently.

As has already been articulated over and over, the subscription business model demands that we pay attention to customers. Not because we want them to be referenceable—although that's nice. Not because we want them to do case studies—although that's nice, too. And not even because our CEOs want to proclaim that they are customer focused—which they will all claim, regardless of whether they practice what they preach. No, this is different. We have no choice but to pay attention to our customers and for one very simple reason—it's life or death. Recurring revenue businesses just can't survive unless they drive success for their customers, because successful customers do two things: (1) they renew their contracts at a high rate and (2) they buy more stuff from you. It's really is as simple as that. And subscription, or pay-as-you-go, businesses will not survive without those things happening.

To be fair, it's never been OK to not manage and nurture customers. We really do want them to successfully use our products and talk about them to others, to be willing references and do other marketing-related things with and for us. And most companies and CEOs truly want customers to be successful for nonfinancial reasons. It just feels good to have customers deriving real business value from the products we've worked so hard to deliver to them. But it was never about desire; it was about motivation. It's one thing to want your customers to get business value, but it's a whole other matter to have your business's viability at stake.

And this isn't an exaggeration for the sake of making a point. The numbers are inarguable. In the perpetual license software world, a very high percentage of the customer's LTV is collected at the time of the initial sale, perhaps as much as 90 percent. In the subscription economy, it's quite likely that the initial deal is worth less than 10 percent of total customer LTV. Let's take a $25,000 annual contract as an example. Customer lifetime would be projected at 7 years minimum but more likely 10 or more years for a healthy customer. That means that this customer will do nine renewals. Even at an annual growth rate of only 5 percent, the customer will end up spending well over 10 times the value of the initial deal during the lifetime of the relationship. And that doesn't even count the nonrecurring dollars from services and training or the 2nd order revenue impact discussed previously.

Thus, the birth of customer success—an organization designed specifically for the intent of driving value to every customer through the use of your product, resulting in high retention rates and a healthy business. This makes for a pretty simple metric for measuring what these customer success people are accomplishing—net retention. But what are they actually going to do every day?

Relentlessly monitoring and managing customer health, that's what.

Let's tackle each part of that phrase in reverse order.

Customer Health

Even before we define what customer health means, we should answer *the why*. Motivation is almost always derived from the why, not *the what* or *the how*. So why do we care about customer health? The answer probably seems obvious, but let's make it a little bit more concrete. Because sales has been around forever, and most everyone understands how it works, it will serve as our analog. Understanding customer health in the customer success world is very similar to your sales leadership (and executives) understanding their pipeline. And what does a clear vision of the pipeline do for your sales VP? At least three things:

1. Predict future behavior
2. Predict timing of future behavior
3. Enable better management of the team

To put it succinctly—forecasting and management. Customer health for a VP of customer success provides the same value. It's a daily predictor of future customer behavior (renewal, upsell, churn, at risk) and offers a more timely way to manage your team (no need to wait 12 months to find out a CSM's churn/retention rate).

Now, on to the what. What is customer health? Well, the word *health* is no coincidence. It really is akin to our health as human beings. If we go to the doctor and get a thorough physical, we could be given a health score, right? Let's see here—this patient has a normal temperature and heart rate. His blood work reveals no major problems, but his cholesterol is a little bit high. He's also 10 pounds over his ideal weight and exercises only three times a month. We could run a bunch more tests, but those are the usual ones for a man his age. On a scale of 0 to 100, let's give him a score of 84.

Customer health works the same way. We can run a series of tests to determine overall health. Of course, that first requires a definition of *healthy* against which to compare the test scores. It's likely that you have a bunch of healthy customers. You know who they are, and you probably also know why you consider them healthy: they use your product almost every day, even some of the more advanced features. They call your support folks often enough for you to know they are actively using your product, but they don't call too often. They pay their bills on time, and their last customer satisfaction survey score was 90. You can determine customer health anecdotally or scientifically. Ultimately, it will probably be a combination of both, but you need to tackle it in some way. Every company is different, so there's no one way to do this, but here's a list of possible customer health components that could be used to determine overall health:

- **Product adoption:** If you can get this data, do so. It will be of great value in determining customer health. Look at it in every possible way: How often do customers use the solution? Are they using your stickiest features? How many people are using it? Do executives use it? Is it used in board meetings, executive meetings, departmental meetings, and the like? Nothing will tell you more about your customers' health than whether and how they use your product. However, there's more to customer health than this. If you don't have access to product usage data, the rest of this list will be even more important.

- **Customer support:** How often does the customer call? How long is the average case open (how many Priority 1 cases vs. Priority 2 or 3, etc.)? Good, healthy customers usually call or use support with some regularity. This is a good indicator of customer health.
- **Survey scores:** Think about customer relationships as human relationships. Both verbal communication and nonverbal communication are important, but what your customers tell you directly when asked is critical.
- **Marketing engagement:** What happens when you send the customer a marketing e-mail? Does it bounce? Does the customer unsubscribe? Does the customer open, click through, or download? What happens is revealing, no matter the outcome.
- **Community involvement:** If you have a community, your customers, regardless of health, probably spend time there. What they do can be very interesting. Are they asking questions or answering them? Do they submit product requests? Do they vote on proposals from others?
- **Marketing participation:** Do your customers provide references for you? Case studies? Speak at your conferences? Healthy customers do.
- **Contract growth:** A customer's investment in your technology and services is a clear indicator of loyalty. If after five years a customer's contract is the same size as at the outset (or smaller), the customer is probably not as healthy as one whose contract has doubled.
- **Self-sufficiency:** Customers who don't need you to help them use your product more effectively are usually healthier than those who rely on you to drive them forward.
- **Invoice history:** Healthy, happy, and loyal customers pay their bills on time. Period.
- **Executive relationship:** How good your personal relationship is with each customer, together with how high up the chain they go, can be a very important component of customer health.

At the very least, you owe it to yourself to think through what customer health means and analyze its various aspects for your particular customers. You might make a list like this and then determine that some items are too hard to get or that computing a score is too complex. Or you might decide that the only item that matters is product use. That's fine, because you need to start with something you can both do and explain. But keep your list, and make it a running list, because many other aspects of customer health will come to light as you make this a central point of discussion and consideration.

Regardless of what you ultimately decide, the process will be enlightening and beneficial, and by the end of it, you'll be thoroughly convinced that some kind of assessment of customer health needs to be the focal point of your customer success strategy.

Manage

Such a simple word. So much meaning. Let's dig in. This word is at the core of what your customer success team, if you have one, will actually be doing on a daily basis. In fact, if our thesis is true—that an accurate assessment of customer health is a clear indicator of loyalty and a predictor of future customer behavior—then any activities your customer success team undertakes that aren't designed to drive customer health scores up are activities they should probably stop doing. To lean on a sales analogy again, any activities performed by your sales team that aren't either building pipeline or moving opportunities through the pipeline are not good uses of team members' time.

Creating a customer health score is not an academic exercise. It has a clear purpose. But, if done right, it also creates actionable insights for your team to operate on. For example, if you determine that a customer's health score should go down if they give you a low survey score, that low survey score should be acted on in some way to reverse a negative course for that customer. This is exactly what we mean when we say *manage*. Take action. Don't just observe and ponder. Do something! Analytics or insights with no action are largely useless. At the risk of belaboring the sales comparison, it would be like a sales representative reporting that a deal in her pipeline has been at the same stage for 180 days. Observing and reporting this fact does nothing to advance the business. "Move it or lose it" is likely to become the VP's admonition long before 180 days have passed.

Let's go back to establishing a health score by developing the components of an overall score. These components of overall health are extremely important to your individual CSMs, because they provide them with the power to change the overall score. Think about it this way. If all you have is an overall score, how would you, an individual CSM, move that score up for an individual customer? Ah. Umm. Hmm. Make the customer happier? Right. In other words, just go boil the ocean, please.

But let's look at the same challenge when you have a component-based score. Let's say there's a component called *product adoption* that measures the percentage of purchased, active licenses. Now, if you're a CSM and you want to move a particular customer's health score up, and you see that the customer's product adoption score is really low, with only 13 of 100 licenses active, you suddenly have some very specific action you can take. You can be certain that if you get 60 users actively using your product instead of 13, the overall score will go up significantly.

So establish a customer health score, and then manage to it under the assumption that moving health scores upward indicates increased loyalty and the likelihood of future good things—renewals and upsells.

Monitor

Perhaps this is becoming way too obvious, but we've come this far, so let's keep going. To manage customer health, you must monitor it. Technology can play a huge role in all the areas we've discussed, but it's essential for helping you monitor. If you don't have some kind of system for monitoring your customer's health, you'll be stuck analyzing lots of spreadsheets and reports and trying to draw actionable conclusions from them. This is a reasonable way to start down the path of turning this into something much more scientific and systematic. It's actually helpful to experience the pain of doing something manually, to provide the proper motivation for automating it. It's also useful to create processes that are initially not systematized as you work the kinks out and then automate them. No sense in automating if the process isn't reasonably refined. You'll end up just making mistakes faster.

You can't manage something that you are not monitoring, so this is obviously critical no matter how you do it. The three elements of our law that we've discussed so far are equally important. Any one without the other two is not useful—it's folly. So please don't try it.

Relentlessly

And here's the adverb in our phrase. One could argue that it's not as important as the other three because it's simply describing how to do the particular task. After all, monitoring and managing customer health sounds like a really good idea. And it most definitely is. But as a wise man once said, "If it's worth doing, it's worth doing really well." We all agree that what we're discussing here is worth doing, so why not do it really well by being relentless about it? In fact, it would not be hard to argue that if this is not done relentlessly, it may not be worth doing at all. We definitely live in a world of very high urgency on so many things we are doing. But if we agree that driving loyalty (customer success) is fundamental to the long-term viability of the recurring revenue business model, then do we really have any choice but to be relentless about it? Is there any doubt what your CEO's answer to that question would be?

For most of us, daily work activities are like gas in a vacuum. They expand to fill the entire space. If we had nothing else to do, e-mail would likely consume our entire workday. And we'd probably all agree that we wouldn't be very productive if that's all we did. So why not apply the word *relentlessly* here with no qualms? We're talking about something that *must* be done, by people whose accomplishments will be defined by how well it is done. *Relentlessly* seems like the only logical way to proceed.

Perhaps the best way to summarize this law is with the following meme:

Relentlessly. Monitor. And Manage. Customer Health.

Additional Commentary

Customer health is at the core of understanding and managing customers. But it's also important to understand that customer health is not a constant nor is it typically linear when it changes (and it will). It's more like a sine wave than any other geometric progression I can think of. For those of you who, like me, have dealt directly with customers for many years, you'll nod your head when I say that customer health can change as quickly as the weather in Chicago. One minute it's sunny and warm, and the next minute the wind is blowing and the rain is coming down sideways. A certain customer might be very happy with your application and using it in all the ways you want them to. Then, you ship a new release, which breaks a key feature and gives them trouble performing the upgrade. Yesterday, they would have been an awesome reference. Today, not so much. Next week they'll probably be back in a good place, perhaps even better, because of your lightning-like responsiveness to their challenges and great assistance in overcoming them. Understanding this customer health sine wave is really important because it allows you to take advantage of the peaks and perform interventions in the valleys.

High Touch

For high-touch customers, taking advantage of their happy days and intervening in the valleys will both often happen in a one-to-one situation. That's the nature of high touch and what makes it a much simpler model to understand (not necessarily to execute). If I'm the CSM for an account, I'll probably call them directly to ask them if they'll do a reference for us. Worst case is that I'll send a personal e-mail. Similarly, on the downside, I'm almost certainly going to set up a call to walk through and understand their challenges. But don't forget that, even in a high-touch model, you can take advantage of some tech-touch processes. For example, it wouldn't be a bad experience, even for my highest-touch customer, to receive an automated e-mail that looks like it came directly from me, asking them to do a product review and providing the link to take them to the website where they can do that. In fact, it's clearly more efficient, for both my customer and me, to do this via e-mail because of the link I want them to go to. Plus, with the right tools, I have the ability to automate this e-mail to happen only for those customers who haven't done a review yet and whose health score just went over 85 and only if they have no Support tickets open. To maintain my high-touch relationship with them, I might call them personally to thank them when they complete the review or have a templatized e-mail that I send to them for the same purpose.

Low Touch

Remember when we used the phrase *just-in-time*? This law for the low-touch tier of customers is the perfect place to put JIT into practice.

By definition, you can't afford to have regular calls or QBRs with these customers, so you are forced to live in a world where very few touchpoints are regularly scheduled and the vast majority are triggered at just the right time. The scenario I described above with regard to asking a customer to do a review is a perfect example and also perfectly applicable for all three tiers. On the negative side, let's say we survey our customers regularly, and we just received a below-average customer satisfaction score from one of them. I may use that as an opportunity to intervene with the customer and understand the details and follow-up actions via a phone call, or I might do that intervention only if the customer's health score is also below 70. Over time, you'll get better and better at knowing when to intervene and what your expected results in each situation should be. You'll gain knowledge anecdotally, but you can also apply data science where enough data exists, to help you refine your reasons and your timing for intervention.

Tech Touch

Because tech touch is essentially free, it can be easy to overdo it. All of us are inundated with too much e-mail. It's an amazing tool at our disposal, but it can obviously be overused. And because it's the primary vehicle for interaction with this tier of customers, it's particularly vulnerable to overuse. However, there's a reality we can count on that mitigates this danger. If every automated e-mail you send to a customer looks like it comes from his customer success team or from his *personal assistant to success* and includes highly personalized, timely, and relevant information, it will never be perceived as spam, and there will never be too much of it.

If you are relentlessly monitoring and managing customer health, then all your tech-touch interactions with customers will have this flavor and will be typically received with open arms. However, it's vitally important to track deliverability, open rates, click-through rates, and so on to determine whether this is really true and to watch trends moving in the wrong direction.

Customer health is your key predictor of future customer behavior. Be relentless in pursuing it and using it effectively across all customers.

9 | Law 5: You Can No Longer Build Loyalty through Personal Relationships

Author: Bernie Kassar, Senior Vice President of Customer Success and Services, Mixpanel

Relevance

	LOW	MEDIUM	HIGH
B2B SaaS	★	★	★
SUBSCRIPTION	★	★	★
PAY-AS-YOU-GO	★	★	★
B2C	★	★	★
TRADITIONAL	★	★	

Executive Summary

Vendors today realize that they need to systematically create programs that allow for interaction between them and their customers. Most will need to address how to service the largest portion of their customer base in a technically friendly way while reducing the need for human capital–intensive ways of building relationships. This large portion of customers are usually lower-value customers in terms of annual spend commitment, but they are important for overall growth. This is not to say that you will eliminate the need for personal relationships with your customers; it just dictates a need to develop different programs that fit each segment of your customer base accordingly. This has to be done without losing the strong connection between customer and vendor that ultimately breeds loyalty, and changes what is known as a customer–vendor relationship into a mutual partnership.

Depending on your product and service, you will need to decide how to create a customer experience that develops a connection with your company. Once outlined, that customer experience needs to be captured, driven, and continually refined by your customer success team and practices. However, customer experience must be a top company priority; it can't be delivered by individual relationships with your customers or even by a single department. The customer experience that builds the strongest relationship between you and your customer needs to start during the initial sales cycle (which could be interacting with your website or an actual human), and then moves to onboarding, product quality, support, and solution adoption, while having a strong focus on communication between the two entities and your community of customers.

While all this reads like common business practice, most organizations do not have a cohesive plan (key word being *cohesive*) to deliver the optimal customer experience. By having a customer experience blueprint that maps across the entire organization, and a customer success organization that drives the process, a company will now have data points to drive change and help develop stronger relationship across all customers. The data-driven decisions can allow companies to institute change that includes website design and flow, more intuitive product design, and new customer success programs customized to particular sizes of customer organizations, while allowing you to redirect expensive one-to-one human interaction to your highest-value customers.

Businesses scale only when customers scale. For most companies, that means a long tail of *low-value* customers. In aggregate, they are often extremely valuable, but each of them individually is typically not big enough or strategic enough to merit anything approaching white-glove treatment. These are the customers who make up the bottom of your segmentation pyramid under the heading *low touch* or *tech touch*. You have to figure out how to deliver love and value to these customers without much one-to-one interaction. This will bring out both the best and the worst in your product and your company as you learn whether customers will be loyal because of the value they get from your product, not the relationship they have with an individual.

With the advent of the SaaS delivery model, department heads are now empowered more than ever to drive business value through a wide variety of solutions. With lowered dependency on IT involvement to deliver and maintain business applications, the door has been opened for companies of all sizes to evaluate and invest in solutions to improve their department's productivity and effectiveness. This evolution provides a win for both the customer and the vendor, but it does create a need for a different approach to managing customer relationships.

Previously, vendors serviced customers through one-to-one relationships, either maintained by the original salesperson or managed by a separate group of account managers. This model works well if your customers spend a large amount of money with you, and your company can support the high cost structure accompanying this model. But with solution vendors now growing at a rapid clip by selling to smaller companies first and then working their way up the revenue chain, tackling bigger and bigger clients, the old customer relationship model doesn't work until the vendor has reached a certain maturity point and is starting to sell large, annual, recurring revenue deals. A few of the SaaS vendors that started with this selling model include well-known players, such as DocuSign, Cornerstone OnDemand, Marketo, Salesforce.com, SuccessFactors/SAP, and Xactly, while relative newcomers, such as Gainsight, Mixpanel, and Zenefits, have recently hit the scene. The proven players have established themselves as leaders in their space by having superior products and focusing on customer success initiatives as a high priority. Their early success resulted from the tremendous growth of their top-line revenues; however, for sustained long-term growth, all companies must focus on new business as well as customer retention. By applying some of the following principles and processes, you can advance and improve your customer success initiatives, focusing on building stronger relationships between your company and your customers:

- Segment your customers by a particular metric that works for your business.
- Define a customer coverage model based on your segmentation.
- Create customer interaction categories based on your coverage model.
- Establish a cadence for interacting with customers.
- Help connect your customers by building a strong and loyal community.
- Create a customer feedback loop.

Segment Your Customers Using a Particular Metric That Works for Your Business

Each vendor has a target market, and based on its solution(s), the focus can be 100 percent on a particular segment, à la small and medium-sized business (SMB; think Zoho or Zendesk) or selling just to the enterprises (think Workday), or solutions that range the full gamut, including a solution for B2B and B2C (think LinkedIn—solutions for HR recruiting departments and premium memberships for individual consumers). Regardless of what market you service, you will have to segment each of your revenue streams by customer. The segmentation process allows you to determine the most effective coverage model, which in turn will drive your engagement model. Most recurring revenue businesses segment B2B customers by ARR or another similar measurement that helps bucket customers by size or potential opportunity (segmentation will vary from business to business). By segmenting your customers, you can understand how each independent group behaves as a slice within that segmentation. By analyzing these different slices, you will gain a new lens on key trends by segment. You might identify that your larger customers tend to renew more after they reach a certain milestone, while your smaller customers churn at a higher rate; however, if you can get them successful early, they have a higher propensity to buy more solutions or licenses. Segmenting properly and analyzing trends will allow you to adjust your relationship strategy accordingly.

Define a Customer Coverage Model Based on Your Segmentation

Defining a customer coverage model is not one size fits all. Depending on the solutions you provide and the maturity level of your organization, your coverage model will evolve over time. If you are an early stage start-up, your customer success team might be asked to wear multiple hats and deliver onboarding, training, support, and renewals. As your company matures, you will naturally start to create specific departments to handle each functional area.

Once your organization is big enough to have a dedicated customer success team, you will need to decide on your coverage model. If, as a company, your business does not lend itself to building a customer success organization, you can still apply customer success principles through the tech-touch model. The first step in the process is to define how many accounts fall into the following categories of interaction: high touch, low touch, and tech touch (see guidelines under the following section, "Create Customer Interaction Categories Based on Your Coverage Model"). One approach to help understand your segmentation (if you use ARR as the benchmark) is to see where your Pareto principle kicks in, by analyzing where 80 percent of your revenue is coming from. Based on your findings, you can start making judgments about how many accounts you want managed by high-touch versus low-touch CSMs and programs. Once accounts are established by segment, you can more easily decide how many accounts each of your CSMs can manage appropriately. Depending on the complexity of your solution and the customer's willingness to spend, the range for the number of high-touch accounts managed by an individual CSM can vary from 5 to 15 accounts, whereas your low-touch CSMs might be able to manage from 20 to 50 accounts or even many more. This will vary greatly for every company, depending on a number of factors. The guideline provided for high-touch accounts, for example, is for complex solutions that service multiple departments or the whole company and that have high ARR value—say, $500,000 or more. The focus of this exercise should be on how much to invest in protecting your current revenue stream (and potential upside growth) from your most valuable customers.

Create Customer Interaction Categories Based on Your Coverage Model

The focus has shifted from a one-to-one relationship to one-to-many relationship. As a vendor servicing a broader set of customers, you need to establish multiple programs for customer engagement. These programs should provide a channel to make your customer feel connected to your company. Moreover, these programs should be educating your customers about features and functions but, more importantly, teaching best practices with the goal of increasing overall adoption. Depending on how you categorize your customers into segments, the following guidelines help determine how and when to interact with your customers.

High Touch
- Multiple in-person meetings during a quarter (depending on each customer's initiatives)
- QBR meetings
- Creation of a blueprint success plan
- One-to-one meeting(s) with your executive staff

Low Touch
- One in-person meeting per quarter (or as needed)
- Focus on at least one high-value meeting per month via online or video conferencing
- One-to-one meeting with your executive staff

Tech Touch
- Webinar-style one-to-many customers meetings on product adoption
- Monthly to quarterly newsletter
- Data-triggered e-mail campaigns
- On-demand training and guidance
- Community portal

These are some suggested guidelines, but it will take individual judgment to know where CSMs should be spending time and effort based on the health of their portfolio of customers. Each company will need to define what high-, low-, and tech-touch interactions look like. Depending on your customer mix and spend, you could very well have a high-touch interaction model that does not justify face-to-face meetings and one-to-one executive interaction—and that's okay. If you sell to the SMB market, for example, you might want to consider one executive interaction with many customers. This experience can be delivered through executive roundtable events by region. The key is to have distinct interactions by grouping that are valued by your customer base and provide the right level of attention for each category.

Establish a Cadence for Interacting with Customers

Now that you have segmented your customers by their appropriate *touch* category, you should weave those interactions into your larger communication/relationship strategy. Your goal should be to interact with your customers on at least a monthly basis via your macro-communication strategy (company and product newsletters, regional user groups, annual customer user conference, etc.). The macro-communication strategy should be focused on all your customers (content might vary by segment), but the medium of delivery is the same for all. When you establish your macro-communication strategy for the year, your customer success leader and your CSMs can now layer in the different "touch" interactions for their portfolio of customers.

Now that you have established a macro-communication strategy and an engagement model, you should map out your plan for the whole year. By building your macro-communication calendar, the frequency of inter-action by your "touch" programs becomes much clearer to deliver by your organization and individual CSMs.

Help Connect Your Customers by Building a Strong, Loyal Community

After establishing your customer success coverage model, macro-communication strategy, and cadence of interaction, you have now completed a great portion of your company's plan to stay connected with your customers. The plan should allow for an interactive relationship between your two entities. However, in today's world of highly connected customers (think social media—LinkedIn, Twitter, Facebook, etc.), you need to provide forums for customers to interact with one another. This is going to happen with or without you, so you are better off making it easy for your customers to meet, to collaborate, and to share their experiences. This can be done via electronic means such as a customer portal, or through high-touch gatherings such as regional user groups, meet-ups, or conferences sponsored by your company or an ecosystem of partners. By embracing a customer community and proactively planning a strategy for your customer community, you provide a platform for your users to engage, exchange knowledge, and ultimately build relationships that you helped foster. Most companies believe in a customer community. This is not a new concept, but proactively planning what you want your customers to experience within the community can be a game changer. Your customers are hands down your best marketing and lead source vehicle. You can espouse how great your company and products are until the cows come home, but when your customers do the talking on your behalf, they become your *company success agents* and can convert more users faster by talking about their success. These company success agents help other customers become stronger while delivering your company's value proposition to current and future customers. This role becomes as valuable as (if not more valuable than) your CSMs. It's a Catch-22, though: you need a company that invests in customer success initiatives and/or CSMs to create this new category of company success agents.

Develop a Customer Feedback Loop

To build and foster strong customer relationships and loyalty, you need to create a feedback loop. This strategy can be delivered through surveys, an electronic suggestion box, customer focus groups, one-to-one meetings, or a customer advisory board. You can employ one or all of these mechanisms, but the bottom line is that your customers need ways to voice their opinions on your product strategy, quality, customer support, enablement programs, company vision—or just to provide general feedback.

This feedback is critical to your company's future success and should help drive your current and future initiatives. Companies that listen to their customers get more great product ideas that assist with adoption and allow for stronger loyalty. You need to provide multiple communication channels focused on different goals. These goals should span feedback on specific product and service delivery to your company strategy and future initiatives.

At the end of the day, your customers are the ones fueling your growth and generating your revenues—it seems fair to provide them with a seat at the table—and the most successful SaaS companies provide them an opportunity to sit at the head of the table more often than not.

By now, you probably realize that communication is the key element in building an effective relationship with your customers. To strengthen your customer relationships and to build loyalty in this new era of recurring revenue businesses, follow three basic principles with your communication efforts: (1) communicate often, (2) set clear expectations, and (3) be as transparent as possible. As a vendor, you have now taken on the responsibility of providing a quality product that delivers business value. At the same time, you've taken on the responsibility for deliverables that an internal IT team used to handle, including application availability and uptime, performance monitoring, and delivering easy-to-use products with relevant and timely new features and bug fixes.

For most vendors, the days of selling only multi-million-dollar deals and throwing bodies at the relationship part of account management are long gone. In today's world, we can't afford that level of touch with most of our customers. But this is actually a good thing: all vendors, from SaaS to subscription-based to pay-as-you-go to even B2C, now have the ability (if they choose) to reach all types of customers, from small to large. However, the economics of these deals differ greatly and therein lies your challenge. The way you build your customer success strategy has to mirror the value received from the customer and vice versa. These initiatives will still include some account management for your high-value customers, but your other customer success programs need to address the majority of your customer base and deliver value while being cost-effective.

Solid customer relationships and loyalty are the bloodline of any successful customer success–centric organization. The correlation between strong renewal rates and exceptional customer satisfaction scores depends on your customer's experience. This relationship is no longer owned by an individual but rather by the broader organization. Your whole company now needs to contribute to building the relationship between you and your customers. The relationship is now defined by the products you design, build, market, deliver, and service. By rethinking how you build a relationship with your customers based on the preceding variables, you now have the ability to plan and collaborate with the appropriate parts of the organization to help contribute content and value for all your customer success initiatives.

Additional Commentary

The world of B2B customer relationships has changed dramatically. Back in the days of enterprise software, not so long ago, every relationship with every customer was personal and personalized. There were no such things as e-mail campaigns or communities or even webinars for the most part. It was all about building personal relationships with every customer, and those personal relationships were one of the primary reasons for the loyalty of the customer to the vendor. To be fair, no vendor survives for long if its product doesn't actually do what it promised. But it was the personal relationship established by the sales rep and/or account manager that often kept the customer loyal. Relationships led to referenceability and to additional purchases. Sales skills and product functionality were important, too, but the people part was critical.

As we explored in Chapter 1, the delivery model we call SaaS started to change this equation because it allowed for the expansion of the market for any product into those customers who could not afford million-dollar price tags but could stomach $45,000 a year. And, over time, the price point went down and down and, for some volume B2B products and for all B2C products, the cost of acquisition became extremely low, often free as a starting point (5 GB of storage on Dropbox, for example). This changed the concept of driving loyalty through relationship. Today, this opportunity does not exist except for certain high-price-point companies or the highest tier of customers for most others. Thus, the challenge of building loyalty without creating personal relationships.

High Touch

Actually, this law does not apply, for the most part, to this tier of customers. By definition, relationships are established with high-touch customers. In many ways, this is no different from the enterprise software days. That's why the account managers of the 1990s easily transitioned into high-touch customer success manager roles in the 2000s. There are many elements of managing a high-touch SaaS customer that are very different from enterprise software, such as the inability to customize (configure yes, customize no) the solution in the way that was common with the previous generation of software. But the relationship part of the equation has remained largely the same. Having said that, almost anything you learn and perfect along the lines of tech touch can be applied to your highest tier of customers, too. It may not change the value of the personal relationship but there's nothing wrong with automating some interactions so that one-to-one time can be spent on the most strategic discussions.

Low Touch

This tier is where this particular law starts to apply. As we've talked about many times already, the need for touching customers in a one-to-many way is becoming paramount for success for most product vendors. The JIT model is designed for just this purpose, delivering success with a minimum of personal interaction. Although a customer may very well have a designated CSM in this tier and even know the CSM by name, the relationship as a loyalty-driver will be tenuous at best because of the volume of customers typically managed by the CSM and the need to automate many of the touchpoints.

Tech Touch

This set of customers is the ultimate example of why this law is on our list. When you get to the point as a vendor in which certain customers do not pay you enough to profitably get any kind of one-to-one touches, then loyalty has to obviously come in some other way. One way is to deliver customer success practices through all of your one-to-many vehicles. Fortunately, there are many at your disposal as outlined above:

- E-mail
- Webinars
- Community
- User groups
- Events

The most important one-to-many channel for building loyalty is a subtle one, and we'll talk about that in the next chapter.

It is paramount that customer success–centric organizations become highly skilled at delivering success to their customers without building personal relationships. For volume B2B businesses and for all B2C businesses, there's no choice. This is a world largely unexplored but will mature quickly because the viability of your business absolutely demands it. Ultimately, you must learn to win by building value, not relationships.

10 | Law 6: Product Is Your Only Scalable Differentiator

Author: Kirsten Maas Helvey, Senior Vice President of Client Success, Cornerstone

Relevance

	LOW	MEDIUM	HIGH
B2B SaaS	★	★	★
SUBSCRIPTION	★	★	★
PAY-AS-YOU-GO	★	★	★
B2C	★	★	★
TRADITIONAL	★	★	★

Executive Summary

The key to customer retention, client satisfaction, and scaling the support and service organizations is a well-designed product that's combined with a best-in-class customer experience. Consumer technology has changed the way we work, as well as our customers' expectations. To ensure you have created a product that meets the needs and expectations of your customers, create a client experience team that focuses on building out programs in a client engagement framework—one that drives community among clients, encourages engagement at all levels and roles of the customer base, and provides clear feedback loops that inform product improvements.

Product advisory councils (PACs) and communities of practice (COPs) for functional business process areas are useful programs a client experience team can utilize to drive continuous improvement in all functions, improve the customer experience, and influence product design directly. Both PACs and COPs provide input into the software life cycle development process by communicating business value for product features, which is critical for building a best-in-class offering. A product that is easy to use and that becomes essential to the way people do business will create happy and loyal customers.

CSMs often work 12-hour days, fielding every question under the sun from clients as well as internal colleagues even when it has nothing to do with the CSM's responsibilities. They are the one-stop shop for dealing with customer challenges and questions all day, every day. Even when CSMs are talking to happy customers, it is usually about driving value by getting them to try out a new feature, encouraging more people to use the product, measuring the ROI, and more. A CSM's priorities typically focus on:

- Driving adoption and value of your products
- Fixing root causes of dissatisfaction, such as addressing problems across the client life cycle and support functions
- Making sure your product is best in its class

Ultimately, the key to customer retention, client satisfaction, and scaling the support and service organizations is a well-designed product or solution married with a best-in-class customer experience.

To ensure you have created a product that meets the needs of your customers, create a client experience team that focuses on building out programs in a client engagement framework. This framework is designed to drive community among clients, encouraging engagement at all levels and

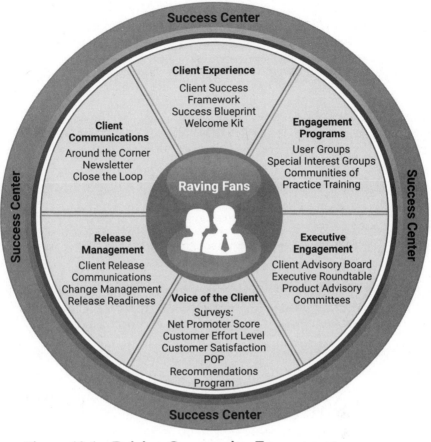

Figure 10.1   Driving Community, Engagement, and Feedback Loops

roles of the customer base, and providing clear feedback loops to drive the CSM's priorities. The framework also allows clients to know that you have an organized way to approach client success management. Each program should have a set objective and key metrics for determining success (see Figure 10.1).

Metrics and analytics derive actionable insights that help drive CSM priorities or tech-touch customer success practices. You will be able to clearly identify drivers of satisfaction and dissatisfaction if you have a defined measurement process and focus on key metrics such as customer satisfaction, NPS, and customer effort–level score (see Figure 10.2).

Typically, the main root of customer dissatisfaction is the product. Simply put, the harder your product is to use, the harder it will be to make your

Customer Satisfaction (CSAT)
Customer (or overall) satisfaction. Most often measured on a 5-point scale but can vary. (Key is the ability to benchmark against historical data.) Used in both transactional and relationship surveys.

Net Promoter Score (NPS)
Measures loyalty, not satisfaction, via willingness to recommend. Always uses an 11-point scale from 0 to 10. Score calculated by subtracting the percentage of 0-6 ratings from the percentage of 9 and 10 ratings. Mostly relationship.

Customer Effort Level Score (CES)
Relatively new metric assessing ease of doing business with a company, measured on a 1-7 scale of agreement. Metric tracked is percentage of respondents who at least "somewhat agree" that handling issue was easy. Mostly transactional.

Figure 10.2   You Can't Manage What You Don't Measure

client successful. We develop products that address business problems, but the goal of a customer success–centric company is to help our customers derive value from those products. Creating a great product that puts design front and center will allow everything else in the customer's experience to flow more easily, making it easier to provide service and support and easier for you to help customers deliver value.

Focus on making the product intuitive. If your customer discussions are constantly about functionality and how to use existing features, you're missing out on the opportunity to drive value-added activities. If a person has to spend a lot of time to figure out the product, it will be less sticky and people will not want to use it. To start, take cues from how people are used to interacting with their favorite apps in their everyday lives. Put yourself in their shoes.

For example, there are norms about how people search for things and what search results look like. We take for granted that we can easily look anything up and do not have to work hard to do so. Give your search information-rich functionality, so users can find what they're looking for when and where they need it and in the way they are accustomed to.

In addition, people want the ability to figure out and fix issues should they arise. Build in self-diagnostic tools to help users find answers themselves and guide them to what they need to be doing. Understand that consumer technology has changed the way we work. We are no longer tied to a desk using a single PC; we use a variety of devices to get work done. Your product's design must support quick access to information and easily executable activities on a mobile device, be it a smartphone, tablet, or even a watch.

The best way to ensure that feedback is getting back to product and other teams, such as sales, services, and customer support, is to have clearly defined feedback loops for the voice of the client. PACs and COPs for functional business process areas are useful ways to drive continuous improvement in all functions, improve the customer experience, and influence product design directly.

PACs provide a structured, interactive platform for clients to engage with your company's product management team by providing feedback and influencing future product direction. The focus of the PACs should be

- To help you define the vision and strategy for your products, understanding the actual business problems your clients face now and into the future
- To discuss how your clients view your products' approach to those problems
- To take into consideration the market and technology trends that your clients see and what their effects might be
- To help you with functional prioritization at a strategic level

The PACs should be led by the product management team (see Figure 10.3).

The roles and responsibilities of a PAC member should be described clearly, with membership criteria determined as the members are representing the larger client base. For example, customer responsibilities might include:

- Actively engaging in PAC meetings and discussions, focusing on strategic business drivers
- Engaging and acting on behalf of peers and the broader client base
- Maintaining a high level of knowledge about current and future product road maps
- Engaging in project-specific design discovery and previews
- Participating in a reference program and speaking positively with clients or prospects on request

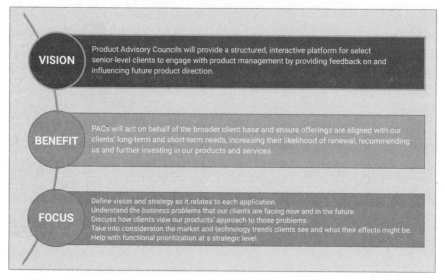

Figure 10.3   **Why Product Advisory Councils**

Example PAC membership criteria could include:

- Senior leader– or executive-level participation to drive strategic product vision
- PAC members to complete an application for PAC
- Members to commit to active participation in the PAC for one calendar year
- Members to commit to attending five meetings per calendar year:
    - Three quarterly road map review and prioritization meetings
    - Two feature request prioritization meetings (by PAC member or delegate)
- Member may not delegate responsibility for quarterly road map review and prioritization meetings
- Member to participate in a reference program, speaking positively with clients or prospects on request

A clear structure and cadence are critical to ensure the value of a PAC for your organization as well as for your clients. It is critical that you continuously highlight to the PAC and the larger client base their influence on product design and road map, to give credence to the voice of the client. A good practice is to send a quarterly communication that shares the

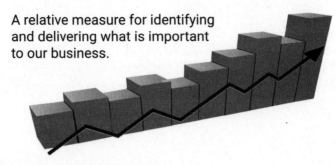

A relative measure for identifying
and delivering what is important
to our business.

Figure 10.4   Business Value

product changes requested by clients, as well as organizational and process improvements that you have made in response to client feedback.

COPs operate much like PACs but really serve as a forum to discuss business processes, practices, and challenges relating to specific products. COPs provide a collaborative forum in which clients are connected with other peers across a variety of business sectors. They tend to be larger groups than PACs.

Both PACs and COPs provide input into the software life cycle development process by communicating the business value of features for the product. The development team should have a defined business value model, based on your business, for use in assessing new features. Partnership with product management and product development in client programs is critical to building a best-in-class product (see Figure 10.4).

Client programs are great ways to ensure that product is the priority and that your product is meeting the needs of clients and the market. Just as critical as client feedback is an organizational focus on client success. Company culture must be ingrained with customer success at its core. It must start from the top and move down, originating with the CEO and senior leadership. Every person in the company has a job because of two things: the product and the customers. The company culture must strive to make each of those a priority. You must turn your customers into raving fans. Create a common set of beliefs that describe your client focus. Ensure that one of your company's goals is a focus on customers. Every department in the company should then have goals aligned with customers. The company should define a customer success framework that clearly outlines the customer journey and what that journey looks like. Employees

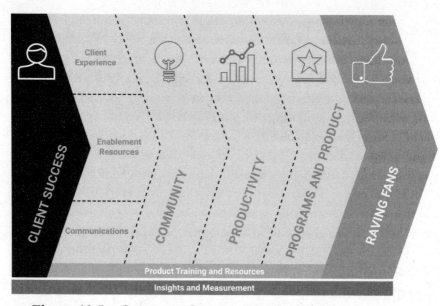

Figure 10.5   Customer Success Framework

need the forums to funnel feedback to all departments, especially product management (see Figure 10.5).

Just like clients, employees who are on the front line, especially if they are real-life users of your product, need a way to deliver feedback on all aspects of the product. The best way to obtain the feedback is to use a similar framework to that used for clients and to define clear channels for employees to submit and discuss product and process enhancements. Employees are a key input that make your product best in its class. Sales, implementation, and customer support input provide a holistic view on what works and what doesn't.

A great way to obtain a fresh perspective is to collect feedback from new employees on the product and the processes that surround the product. Make this a key part of onboarding. Provide new employees with the opportunity to learn the product and to provide feedback to product and process owners, including sales, implementation, and customer support. Always try to have employees walk in the client's shoes. Your best reference is using your own product.

Customer success focuses on helping people deliver results and ROI through products; good design enables that focus to be on value-added activities and not on functionality. Products that become onerous to manage, administer, and use will risk abandonment because customers will not value them. Customer success teams interact with customers every day and are intimate with how your product is being used. A feedback loop between them and your product team is essential.

Switching costs now are much lower than they used to be. As a vendor, all you have is the quality and function of your product combined with the value of the services and support offerings you put around your product. And that support manifests from having a great product that's easy to use. Many vendors get hung up on building in "nice to have," forward-looking features, but often the customer's internal processes are not mature enough to take advantage of such features. The product itself must offer a runway that enables processes to change to accommodate advanced functionality. An easy-to-use product is the basis for getting customers ready for advanced functionality. Bridging that disconnect is critical.

If you've got a product that becomes essential to the way people are doing business and it's easy to use, your customers will be happy and loyal; they'll get the value. If not, they will look elsewhere.

A well-designed product that enables self-sufficiency and delivers value is crucial to customer success. It will not only build loyalty but also enable your team to have more meaningful discussions with your customers and drive further growth.

Additional Commentary

The only really scalable part of your entire company is your product. To be sure, every part of every company can get more efficient and more scalable, but, for every product you create, you have the chance to make it once and have it used millions of times by millions of users. "Make once, ship many" is a recipe for profit if you can get there. Think about it this way. If you made a perfect product (and I mean truly perfect in every way), how many people in your company would be unnecessary? In a typical company, you'd be able to eliminate all of the teams that do any of the following:

- Provisioning
- Implementation

- Training
- Customer support
- Customer success
- Operations
- Professional services (most of, at least)
- Renewals

In other words, you wouldn't even have a concept of *post-sales* because the only thing that would happen post-sales is millions of customers using and loving your product and looking for a way to tell the rest of the world about it.

The B2C world operates with this reality at all times, especially when their applications go to mobile. Look at Google and Facebook as perfect examples. Nobody is assigned to help you install and start using Facebook or to hold your hand while you do your first Google search. It's not necessary because the products are elegant, simple, intuitive, and compelling because they provide tremendous value. For Google and Facebook, the move to mobile definitely raised the ease-of-use bar (not that anything could get much easier than a blank search box), but they benefited from most users having first used their product on a computer. But for companies whose first, or only, product channel is a mobile device, the challenge goes up significantly. Hundreds have figured it out, and thousands more will, too.

The primary reason for making your product priority one across all parts of your company is that it is *the* only path to the wild success you want to enjoy. Mature and successful companies usually create an identity beyond just their culture. Apple's identity is in building beautiful and elegant products. Zappos's identity is in providing the ultimate customer support/customer experience. Walmart's identity is value and convenience. But each of these company's success is tied to creating the best product in their market. One could argue that this is a chicken-and-egg debate. Is Zappos the dominant vendor in the online shoe market because of their customer support? Or is their customer support actually part of their product? Ultimately, for the purpose of this discussion, that doesn't really matter. The bottom line is this: the dominant vendor in virtually every market is the vendor who builds the best product. If a vendor convinces the world (or their market) that the best product isn't just what you touch and use but also the services and support that surround it, more power to them. Great companies do this really well. But, without exception, great companies, above all else, build great products. Any attempt to join the customer success movement without making your product your top priority will be fruitless in the long run.

High Touch

For companies whose primary customer success model is high touch or who have a tier of high-touch customers, the key to becoming product focused is communication. In particular, communication between your customer success team and your product team. CSMs are on the front lines in this situation and know more about how your product is being used or is wishing to be used than anyone else in your company. It's healthy to think of them as field product managers to embrace this truth. The value of all that knowledge is realized only if it transfers from the CSMs to the Product Managers (PM). As a company, you need to design processes to ensure this is happening. If I'm managing 40 CSMs and telling them that product is their first priority, even while they spend 12 hours a day helping solve customer challenges, I better create a communication process that makes it easy for them to share the experiences of their customers with the PM team. Of course, there should also be a way for customers to communicate this directly, but the CSM filter will be vital. It could start simply with a monthly meeting between customer success and product in which the customer stories are shared. This isn't particularly scalable, but it's a good way to start. Part of the purpose of this team could be to figure out a scalable process. It's important, within this process, to capture the business problems, not just the request for features. Perhaps most important will be understanding what problems they'd like your product to be solving for them in the future. This will help drive some step-function improvements, not just incremental change.

Low Touch

As you move down the touch model you obviously need to create even more scalable processes. In particular, you'll probably want to make it easier for customers to communicate their needs and frustrations with your product, directly to the PM team. You can use communities, forums, surveys, and user groups to accomplish this at scale. A community, or forum, using the social media construct of voting or like/dislike can work really well if you have enough participation and can ensure that the product elements being voted on are clear. As mentioned earlier, a handpicked PAC or customer advisory board (CAB) can be extremely valuable if they are a good cross section of your customer base. Don't invite only enterprise customers to your CAB if 70 percent of your business is SMB. You might think about having two different CABs in a situation where the markets and use of your product are very different in each segment. The lower touch your model is, the more important it is to get your product right so you absolutely need to find a way to do this with your customer's involvement. You certainly won't have armies of services and customer success people to work around product deficiencies.

Tech Touch

In a B2C or volume B2B market, everything needs to be driven through technology, as we've stated many times. However, that doesn't mean you can't still talk to customers and get some direct feedback. It's useful to do this whether it's through a user group or a focus group. But your primary vehicles will be the one-to-many ones, such as communities, forums, and surveys. Because of the volumes involved here, the most useful feedback probably comes directly from your product. The parts used most often are telling. The places where more time is spent could be important, either positively or negatively. You can build some limited feedback mechanisms into your product to collect data as the customer is experiencing it. It's no stretch to think that the best direction on where to go with your product lies in how it's being used today. Volumes of users also make experimentation pretty easy and very valuable. You can add a feature for a day and see what the results are. This is certainly happening every day on sites like Amazon, eBay, and Match.com.

Okay, the drum has been beaten loudly enough. Prioritize your product or customer success will be elusive at best and you will fail as a company. And, if you have people touching your customers in any way, shape, or form, make sure that they realize that the quality and value of your product is their top priority, too.

11 | Law 7: Obsessively Improve Time-to-Value

Author: Diane Gordon, Chief Customer Officer, Brainshark

Relevance

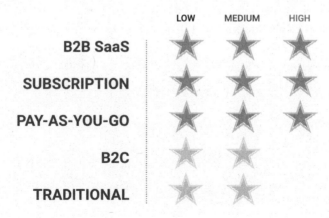

Executive Summary

Why do people or companies buy? They think they'll get value from their purchase. If you're a consumer, this might mean spending a lot of money at a fine restaurant because you hope to get an above average meal. And you find out pretty much right away: it's either delicious or so-so. Based on that, you can decide whether you'll ever return.

But when you are selling business products and services, it's often tough to show value that close to the transaction. Although buyers know this, they do expect to see value in a reasonable time frame. For SaaS or subscription-based vendors, that time frame is the length of the subscription. If the customer hasn't seen real value by the time renewal discussions begin, they're far less likely to renew. Working against the vendor is how long it might take to get the customer up and running with the solution. Obsessively improving time-to-value is the way to address this challenge.

A big part of any sales process is convincing prospects that they will get real value from your product or solution. In the world of SaaS or subscriptions, delivering that value quickly is key to retention and expansion. Customers don't renew or stay with you or buy more unless or until you deliver value to them.

If you're implementing enterprise software on a subscription basis, the onboarding process alone can span a few months, leaving only a few additional months of production time in which to see value. That's pretty risky when there's a one-year renewal looming. To highlight this challenge, consider the extreme: if it takes 11 months to get a customer up and running and the contract is 12 months long, are the odds of renewal better or worse than if the customer had been live in 60 days (see Figure 11.1)?

There's clearly a direct correlation between the length of onboarding and the likelihood of the first renewal. If you are in a pay-as-you-go business in which all contracts are monthly, it's even more critical.

What's the secret to ensuring that the customer sees value as quickly as possible after buying your solution?

- Work with the customer to establish concrete success measures.
- Implement iteratively for early value, achieving the simplest measure first and focusing on the others later.
- Adjust in real time, springing into action the very moment you realize expected value is at risk.

Let's look at each of these points in a bit more detail.

Establish Concrete Success Measures

Ideally, your customers made a buying decision based on the value of your product or solution. Even more, they know how they're going to measure that value.

Work with the business sponsor to define measures early. It is critical to leverage business sponsors while you have their attention during the sales process, because they will likely be less involved in the tactics of the implementation itself. Trying to get the business sponsor's attention later in the customer life cycle is difficult, after they have moved on to other things. Taking advantage of the opportunity to have the business sponsor's focus earlier on is the best way to capture success measures that resonate at the business level of the organization.

If you're lucky, the customer will have a concrete answer: "We want to cut in half the time it takes to onboard a new representative." But much more often, while customers might have cited key drivers, they don't have specific measures in mind (and if they do, they don't know what the baseline values of those measures are today). In this case, rather than asking the customer to come up with metrics (something that can take a while, especially in a complex organization), we present a list of the measures our customers typically use to gauge success:

- Decreased time to reach quota.
- Increased number of representatives meeting quota.
- Increased number of converted marketing leads.
- Increased deal size or revenue.

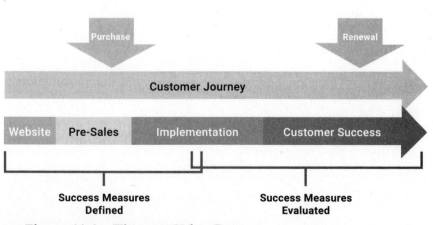

Figure 11.1   Time-to-Value Process

- Increased percentage of representatives actively using Salesforce.
- Increased amount of time representatives spend selling versus searching for content.
- Decreased time to onboard representatives.
- Decreased time to close first deal.
- Decreased time managers spend coaching representatives.
- Increased representative competency with material.
- Increased number of representatives who fully complete onboarding curriculum.
- Increased viewership (number of views).

We ask the customer to choose from these examples, making sure that they have baseline values for any measure(s) they choose.

You should also communicate these measures to the onboarding team. One process that works well is to have the success measures documented by the pre-sales team and then pass those on to the onboarding team at the beginning of the implementation process. Then, during the onboarding kickoff call, the pre-sales engineer validates those measures with the customer: "During the sales cycle, you indicated that decreased employee onboarding time was a key driver. Is that still true? If so, how long does onboarding take today?"

It is only after these success measures are clearly defined that we start the onboarding clock. Otherwise, you may find yourself months into an onboarding program—or, worse, fully implemented—without the customer knowing whether they've gotten any value from your solution.

You can also create a positive carryover effect with these concrete metrics. If you do QBRs or some kind of regular reviews with your customers, you can revisit these metrics frequently (1) to determine whether they are still the right metrics for the business and (2) to validate your success against those metrics. Many customers seem to shy away from measuring hard ROI, despite having often been adamant about it during the sales process. But you know it will come back to bite you if you don't help the customer measure it.

Implement Iteratively for Early Value

Don't boil the ocean. The fastest way to get to value is to begin meeting those most easily achievable criteria. For example, customers that buy a solution to improve sales productivity might use two or three (or more) success measures: decreased time to onboard sales representatives, more effective prospect engagement, and increased percentage of representatives hitting quota.

Although these are all achievable, the customer will see value more quickly by starting with the most important measure. Do this through an iterative implementation process, focusing on, say, training and onboarding times in Phase I and improving prospect engagement in Phase II (see Figure 11.2).

There are other ways to get to quicker value as well, for example, rolling out to specific groups, divisions, or geographies rather than an entire user population, or focusing on one or two specific initiatives (e.g., rebranding) or product lines. Slicing the challenge into small achievable chunks and implementing iteratively produces value early and often.

Also, confirm constantly. Don't make the mistake of assuming that just because the business sponsor defined metrics during the sales cycle and the customer's project team validated those metrics, they will remain the ones that matter:

- List the measures at the top of every status report and call attention to them during every check-in call: "Just checking in—these are still the measures that we care about for this phase, right?"
- At multiple points during the onboarding, connect directly with the business sponsor to validate the measures.

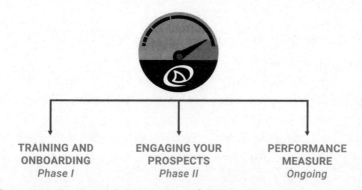

TRAINING AND ONBOARDING
Phase I

ENGAGING YOUR PROSPECTS
Phase II

PERFORMANCE MEASURE
Ongoing

Figure 11.2   Iterative Implementation Example

Adjust in Real Time

As the end of an onboarding program nears, introduce the CSM and/or your customer success practices, bringing her into project status calls and educating her about the selected success criteria. The CSM's highest priority in the weeks and months after onboarding is to be obsessive about ensuring that the customer achieves the stated value. All other traditional customer success activities (introducing new features, doing quarterly business reviews, etc.) take a back seat to this critical item.

Why is this so important? Well, we find that once customers finish onboarding, their project team may lose focus as its members turn their attention back to their day jobs. When that happens, we assume that the customer just isn't going to be as laser focused on getting to value as we will be. The CSM is responsible for reporting on progress to both the customer and to the larger account management team and, then, reengaging resources as quickly as possible if the value timeline is hitting snags.

Another compelling reason for obsessively driving time-to-value is because we want our customers to have the opportunity to expand our solution. As vendors, we call this upsell. But if we look at it from the customer's standpoint, it's extending the value of her investment in your technology. In a subscription-based world, it's key to grow the customer's overall contract value over time. The process of doing that can only begin once the customer has reached the point at which she is getting real value from your product. No customers will buy more licenses or add-on modules of your product(s) if they aren't yet deriving business value. To assess the magnitude of this, simply multiply 30 days by the number of customers you have. The result is the number of additional selling days you will have available to you because you improved time-to-value by 30 days for the next set of customers. If that's not reasonable, use 5 days as your multiplier. Just calculate a number and ask yourself what a good sales team (yours) could do with that number of additional selling days.

Customers buy because they believe the value will far exceed the cost of your solution. But for subscription businesses, it's simply not safe to assume this will just happen. You have to own making sure your customers know how they'll measure value and that they actually see the measures improve long before that renewal call comes in.

Additional Commentary

The key word in this law is *obsessively*. In general, everyone wants to improve the time it takes to do anything. It's part of our DNA as employees to drive improvement in everything we do. But how many things do we really obsess over? Not that many. This is an area where you need to.

Let's draw a comparison to sales here because great salespeople obsess over getting their deals closed. It's part of what makes them great. When they are driving home on a Friday evening looking forward to the weekend and their phone rings with a call from a prospect, what do they do? They answer it, right? They answer it because they know that every single day in a sales cycle is critical and that there's only one good day to close any deal—today. Every sales rep who has been around for a time can tell you about the one that got away. The deal they had almost signed on a Wednesday only to hear about layoffs, poor earnings, or an organization change on Thursday, which derailed them. Salespeople know about obsessing over every day because every day matters.

Prior to SaaS and subscriptions, the post-sales mentality did not generally include that same level of urgency. After all, in a six-month or longer implementation cycle, how much can one day really matter? The problem with that approach is that, if one day doesn't matter, then two days don't really matter, either, and the death spiral continues. This is not to say that the implementation teams and customers don't care. They most certainly do. But the nature of subscriptions and the always-impending renewal or chance to opt-out dramatically increases the urgency.

In the world of enterprise software, time-to-value is often measured in months because of the complexity of implementing the solutions. If you are selling e-commerce solutions or B2C, time-to-value is still relevant and important, but it may be measured in hours or even minutes. When I set out to download and start using the GoToMeeting mobile app, my expectation is that the whole process should take less than five minutes. That's not a lot of time for anyone so where does the urgency come from to shorten that to four minutes and then three minutes? It comes from one of two places: (1) the end user or (2) WebEx. If you aren't obsessing about time-to-value, no matter what business you are in, your competitors likely are and that will differentiate them. This is especially true in markets as they become commoditized. It's very hard for Citrix to differentiate their GoToMeeting product from WebEx to the general user, which means that everything else matters that much more—price, time-to-value, support, and overall customer experience. Those minutes matter. Obsess over them. Fight for them.

High Touch

Because high touch usually means high value, which almost always comes with higher complexity, we're usually talking about finding ways to shave days or maybe weeks off your implementation process. And although much of time-to-value in this scenario is about implementation, let's not let it get narrowed down to only that. It's not *time-to-implementation*, it's *time-to-value*. For vendors dealing with high-touch clients, your implementation team and your customer success team usually share this responsibility. It's almost never the case that *project complete = value received*. It's a huge step in the process, but there's always more work to do. This is where a CSM starts to earn his keep. Once he has a fully functional solution with which to work, he can engage the customer in starting to use it to solve the business problems for which it was purchased to solve.

One of the challenges created by this handoff is actually measuring when the customer receives value. It's fairly easy to measure how long an implementation project takes. There's a kickoff date and a project completion sign-off date. If the average time between those two dates for your company is 97 days, then you can set a target to bring that down to 89 days next quarter, and 83 the quarter after that. It's pretty easy to measure. But the term *value* is not as concrete, which is why you probably need to create a proxy for it. This usually means determining which parts of your product have the highest value and measuring whether, or how much, each customer is using those features. Or, it could be done via direct interaction with your customers: "Was our product used by every department manager to input their budget numbers for next year?" If the answer to a question like that is yes, assuming that's why they bought your product, then you've certainly reached the point of value. For many companies using the latest technology for customer success management, value could be measured by the customer's health score. Regardless of your method, if you are going to obsess over time-to-value, you need to find a way to determine and measure value. Not doing that leaves your customer success team and your company, hanging out to dry.

Low Touch

The low-touch model actually puts more pressure on time-to-value for many companies. That's because this is usually only a tier of customers, not the focus of the whole company. That means these customers are most likely buying and implementing the same product as your high-touch customers but most likely have not spent as much money on it, aren't staffed in the same way to complete the project, and didn't pay as much for the services portion of the solution. And, in many cases, their expectations are actually higher: "We're a small company compared to some of your other customers. Why does this take so long?"

One possible way to solve this challenge is to be much more rigid and prescriptive with this tier of customers in how the implementation and customer success processes work. You could define each step in the implementation process and define exactly what you will do and what is expected of the customer. When Step 8 is done, so is the project. The same with customer success—handoff call, 60-minute training session, 30-minute follow-up two weeks later, and then quarterly health checks. In between, lots of automated touches that bring valuable content to the customer at just the right time (remember, "just-in-time"?).

This is not usually the way you deal with high-touch, high-value clients, and there's most definitely some risk. But, by definition, you can't spend the same amount of time with these clients, so you have no choice. This also means that the chances of losing these customers are higher, and those expectations should be set throughout your company. It's not feasible to expect the same retention results with reduced time and attention. For all these reasons, automation becomes imperative if for no other reason than to get far more precise at forecasting churn. Again, the development of technology for customer success management can be of tremendous value here.

Tech Touch

Time-to-value still matters for your tech-touch customers as we mentioned earlier. What also matters is the complexity of your product. It's virtually impossible to deliver value quickly enough exclusively through technology, if your product requires more than (1) download, (2) configure, (3) use. But even if it is that simple, you'll need to take advantage of every possible technology trick to make that experience the best one possible for your customers. This is one reason so many consumer apps allow you to login using your Facebook or Google credentials. It shortens the time for a user to actually start using your product by skipping part of the setup/identification process. B2B companies have something to learn from this if only in driving the thinking about how to cut minutes out of the process.

We've also mentioned in-app guidance before, and that is highly applicable here, too. B2C products are often so simple that almost no guidance is required to get started. But B2B products, and some B2C products, are often just complex enough so that some kind of assistance is necessary to get a user through the process. Take Dropbox as an example. Far too many people have downloaded and begun to use it for there to be a team at Dropbox talking users through the process. The entire experience *has* to be technology driven, and it is. The website is set up for the exclusive purpose of walking you through downloading and then installing the product. Icons and messages tell you what is happening along the way, and then the first thing that happens after the install is complete is that a 10-page pdf appears in your Dropbox folder, providing instructions on how to start taking advantage of it. As that's happening, there's also an encouragement on the screen to move your first file into Dropbox. This five-minute experience explains everything we've discussed in this chapter: easy on-screen or in-app guidance to download and then install and, very importantly, pushing you to actually upload your first file. It's clear that the time-to-value clock for Dropbox continues to tick until the first file is uploaded. It doesn't stop when the download or the install is completed.

Obsess about time-to-value. You'll never be sorry you did, regardless of the type of product you deliver or the kind of customers who use it. It's on your critical path to success for your customers.

12 | Law 8: Deeply Understand Your Customer Metrics

Author: Kathleen Lord, Vice President of Sales and Customer Success, Intacct

Relevance

	LOW	MEDIUM	HIGH
B2B SaaS	★	★	★
SUBSCRIPTION	★	★	★
PAY-AS-YOU-GO	★	★	★
B2C	★	★	★
TRADITIONAL	★	★	★

Executive Summary

Successful subscription-based companies must deeply understand the details of churn and retention if they are going to maintain and accelerate their revenue growth. Nothing slows your company's growth rate faster than having revenue from your installed base evaporate. As your installed base revenues grow, even a 1 percent increase in churn can make a huge difference in your company's velocity. If you are at a $25 million run rate and are trying to maintain a 50 percent or more growth rate, a 1 percent increase in churn means your sales team will have to close an extra 20 percent in new business sales to maintain your growth rate. The following five steps will help you define and gain a deep understanding of churn and retention to help your company focus on the right priorities, accelerate growth, and keep your customers for life.

The biggest issue early-stage, subscription-based companies face is how to accelerate customer acquisition. In fact, the majority of a company's resources (time and money) are spent figuring out how to solve this problem and prove that the company has a viable business model. However, as soon as a company has successfully solved the challenge of accelerating customer acquisition, someone—your CEO or a finance person most likely—starts to notice that the company's total customer count and committed monthly recurring revenue (CMRR) are declining.

CMRR is defined as the combined value of all of the recognized recurring subscription revenue on a monthly basis, plus signed contracts currently committed and going into production, minus churn. Churn is the monthly recurring revenue that is no longer committed from customers that have turned off the service or are anticipated to do so in the future. Your sales VP might wonder how this could be, considering that he or she is doing such a great job driving new business. Unfortunately, many companies do not invest enough company resources to successfully retain the customers on whom they've spent a significant amount of the company's resources to acquire. And, as the driving force behind this book, this is exactly how the organization commonly known as customer success came into being.

To sustain a subscription-based company for the long term, your company must have a deep understanding of both churn and retention: churn from the standpoint of understanding why and how often customers leave and retention from the standpoint of why and how often customers stay and continue using your product or service. The earlier in your company's lifecycle churn and retention are addressed, the easier the problem is to solve.

Companies can follow five steps to capture, measure, and understand churn and retention:

1. Define what you are measuring, and components of CMRR.
2. Define the period of measurement and frequency.
3. Determine the expected CMRR and categories of churn.
4. Determine how to identify suspected/at-risk churn.
5. Align with your executive leadership to develop a set of standard definitions and reports for churn/retention.

Step 1: Companies must first define how they are going to measure churn and retention. Does it make more sense to measure on a per-customer basis, on a per-contract basis, or both? This decision will depend a lot on customer size (SMB versus enterprise) and whether your company has multiple contracts that are managed separately under a single customer umbrella (e.g., a company might have five different divisions of GE as customers). In addition, it is fundamental in determining how your company needs to operationalize the way it captures and calculates churn and retention on a go-forward basis. The necessary operational changes include the ability to capture churn and retention both from a CMRR dollar perspective and from a count perspective.

The next step is to determine how you will define CMRR. The typical components of CMRR usually include new CMRR, add-on CMRR, renewal CMRR, and churn. Figure 12.1 is a graphical representation of how each of these components is combined with your period-beginning CMRR to calculate your period-ending CMRR, with the difference being your net change in CMRR. Net change in CMRR is the amount you grew your business period over period, and it provides the clearest forward-looking view into the health of your business.

The best practice is to have an even-more granular view by breaking down renewal CMRR into multiple buckets, including cancellations, downgrades, upgrades, and first-time archives. (Note: many cloud companies offer an archive service at a percentage of the former annual subscription fees to provide ongoing read-only access to the data after a customer is no

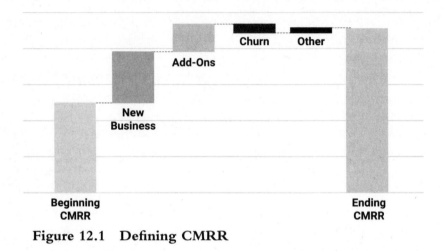

Figure 12.1   Defining CMRR

longer actively using the service.) This granular breakdown of the renewal CMRR provides insight into your renewal business so your company can more effectively pinpoint where there is a potential problem versus just providing high-level churn and retention rate numbers.

For example, let's say the customer had a $50,000 contract that they renewed, and the new contract was worth $55,000. Celebrate, right? Definitely, but not so fast. Let's examine the details:

- $45,000 apples–to–apples renewal of products A and C
- $8,000 churn of product B
- $14,000 upsell of additional licenses for product A
- $4,000 increase because discount went from 25 percent to 22 percent

Somebody cares a lot about each of those line items—the product manager for product B for sure, and your CFO almost certainly. There's no time like the present for figuring out how you are going to track at this level of detail.

Your company will need to build out its order process to capture the necessary data at the level of granularity in which your company wants to be able to report on churn and retention (customer, contract, etc.). This includes capturing order type (new, add-on, renewal), upgrade/downgrade amounts on the renewal (recommended to track actual new product add-ons separately), reasons for downgrade at the stock-keeping unit (SKU) level, and reasons for cancellation. Best practice in your CRM system is to have both a picklist of reasons for ease of standardized reporting, as well as a freeform comment field to capture additional color commentary. Ideally, your company's order process is set up to capture the difference between a quantity downgrade versus a price downgrade, for these are very different churn problems to address.

In addition, having the downgrade/churn reasons automatically populate a churn-type field will greatly facilitate real-time reporting of avoidable versus unavoidable churn. For reference, unavoidable churn is often referred to as *death and marriage.* In other words, churn caused when a customer goes out of business or gets acquired is generally accepted as unavoidable. This will become very important as you begin reporting on your downgrade and churn reasons and prioritize the ones you need to address first. Although most enterprise resource planning (ERP) or customer success applications enable you to track this level of detail through different transaction types, some burden will be placed on your sales and finance operations teams.

Step 2: Once your company has determined the basis against which it is measuring churn and retention, it must determine the period of measurement and frequency of that measurement. Depending on your company's business model, it may make sense to measure churn and retention weekly, monthly, quarterly, or annually. This should be determined by the length of commitment customers are required to make and align with how the company plans CMRR and churn to facilitate comparisons versus plan. Often companies measure churn and retention on a more granular basis—say, monthly—but report these metrics as an annualized rate for key stakeholders. This approach makes it easier for key stakeholders to have a clearer picture of the annualized effects of churn and retention.

In addition, it's important to define how you will handle both early and late renewals relative to the period of measurement. In terms of booking renewals early, this is a very good thing for your company. However, you need to make sure the renewal is booked in the period in which it is due; booking in an earlier period will significantly throw off churn and retention metrics. When handling late renewals, the best practice for keeping your company's churn and retention metrics accurate is to move the expected CMRR and expected customer count to the next period while maintaining the same subscription start and end dates. This approach enables the company to accurately measure churn and retention while also being able to report on late renewals. This is a key metric that the company should measure. Ideally, all renewals are completed 30 to 60 days in advance of their subscription end date.

Step 3: Determining how your company will calculate renewal rates starts with determining how you will define expected CMRR. The best practice for determining expected CMRR is to add the CMRR of the prior-period renewal to the annualized value of any add-ons during the period. This becomes the basis for calculating your company's churn and retention. This approach also means the churn plan you set at the beginning of your fiscal year will change over the course of the year as customers add on incremental subscriptions.

Customer success and finance need to agree on the point in time when your company will lock in your expected CMRR. Best practice is at the beginning of the fiscal period during which the renewal is due (monthly or quarterly). If your customers are highly dynamic (e.g., regular cadence of death and marriage), then you should determine an appropriate churn run rate that is acceptable to your overall business model. For example, if your company determines that planning for a 10 percent churn rate is appropriate, then the original plan will model churn at 10 percent of expected CMRR at the beginning of your fiscal period and will be adjusted at the beginning of each new fiscal period to reflect 10 percent of the revised expected CMRR. Otherwise, midterm add-ons can significantly misrepresent the health of your business and mask potential churn issues. This type of churn is classified as unavoidable; you should build it into your overall bookings and revenue plans so you can provide more predictable forecasts for the business.

For example, calculating expected CMRR at the beginning of your fiscal year as the basis for your company plan might look like this:

- Prior-year renewals = $25 million
- Assumed 10 percent churn (due to death, marriage, etc.) = ($2.5 million)
- Planned expected CMRR = $22.5 million

A moderate approach to account for the annualized value of midterm add-ons is to update the expected CMRR plan at the beginning of each fiscal quarter. For example, you want to calculate updated expected CMRR at the beginning of your second fiscal quarter along these lines:

- Original planned expected CMRR = $22.5 million
- Added annualized value of midterm add-ons from fiscal Q1 = $1.76 million
- Updated planned expected CMRR = $24.26 million

The most conservative approach to accounting for the annualized value of midterm add-ons is updating expected CMRR at the close of each fiscal period (generally monthly if you are doing monthly closes). For example:

- Original planned expected CMRR for September = $1.5 million
- Added annualized value of midterm add-ons for September renewals = $225,000
- Updated planned expected CMRR = $1.725 million

If you have multiple customer segments in your business, you should calculate expected CMRR for each customer segment as part of your planning process, since each segment will usually have a different projected churn rate.

Step 4: An emerging area of focus for many companies is to take a much more forward-looking view of the company by measuring suspected or at-risk churn. There are two ways to forecast suspected churn or at-risk customers: (1) through human interaction and (2) by leveraging signals or data points. In a traditional enterprise, leveraging human interaction is much easier, because the company can typically afford to establish a customer success team. This team engages with customers on a frequent basis and can qualitatively assess and document a customer's likelihood of churn. The challenge with this approach is that as the company's customer success team begins to scale, it becomes harder and harder to maintain objective and consistent qualitative assessments of risk across your CSMs. For companies that sell to the SMB market, staffing a customer success team at low-enough ratios to develop deep-enough relationships to obtain good qualitative churn assessments is not fiscally possible.

Leveraging signals or data points is a great quantitative way to supplement the qualitative assessment from your human interactions in the enterprise model and is a much more cost-effective way of assessing likelihood of churn in the SMB market. The first steps are to define and gain agreement on the attributes of your happiest and healthiest customers and, then, define the attributes for your at-risk customers. These attributes could include use patterns, number of support cases, NPS, tenure, contract growth, or departure of key contacts or sponsors. Although it's certainly possible to try to capture and maintain this type of customer health information in your customer relationship management solution or Microsoft Excel, the company can be much more efficient and proactive by implementing a purpose-built customer success application.

Customer success management applications not only help automate the process of capturing and scoring customer health but also provide a centralized repository that all key customer-facing personnel across the company can access in real time when engaging with customers. In addition, they can provide you with the capability for doing tech touch for some deliverables or some set of customers; that is, driving relevant and timely touching of your customers through automated one-to-many channels instead of the expensive one-to-one processes.

Having a clear, forward-looking view of churn and retention enables the company to forecast much more accurately and to proactively address potential churn issues, both of which are critical to successfully growing your subscription base business.

Step 5: Aligning with executive leadership to develop a set of standard definitions and reports for churn and retention is needed to present key stakeholders with a clear view of the health of the business. The company should be measuring both CMRR and customer count churn and retention by the dimensions relevant to the company's business, for example, understanding churn and retention by industry, size, customer tenure, geographic region, sales channel, product line, or CSM, both from a CMRR perspective and a customer count perspective. To easily create these reports, the company needs to capture these dimensions at the level of granularity in which the company wants to measure churn and retention. Being thoughtful early on about the data you want to be able to report on, and setting your systems up to capture this information, provides the company with strategic insight on churn and retention that can help the company accelerate growth.

In addition, making these reports available to the executive on a consistent basis with changes over time highlighted enables the company to identify what needs to be addressed. Just as importantly, the reports highlight the impact of new programs and processes that have been rolled out. For example, product development and engineering need to understand prioritization of enhancements that will have the biggest impact on customer success.

Perhaps a segment of your customer base is consistently unsuccessful, and the sales team needs to be advised not to close more customers matching that profile. Or customers are consistently not getting the training they need to achieve long-term success. Understanding churn and retention at a very granular level can help guide every facet of the company with regard to focus, priority, and investment to accelerate performance and growth.

Figure 12.2 shows an operational-level dashboard available from the Gainsight customer success management application to help your company proactively manage churn and retention.

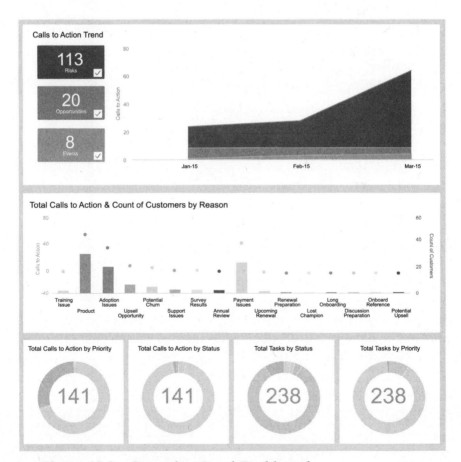

Figure 12.2   Operation-Level Dashboard

Intacct.

Dashboards | Reports | Company | General Ledger | Time & Expenses | Cash Management | Accounts Receivable | Order Entry | Accounts Payable | Purchasing | Projects | Inventory Control | Platform Services | Payroll Import

Winifer ▼   Help ▼

Digital Board Book - SaaS Metrics

▼ Clear | As of today | All departments | All locations

CMRR per Customer
$14,674
↑
prior year   +$557 vs. prior period

CMRR
$5.40M
↑
prior year   +$1,166,000 vs. prior period

Customer Renewal
98%
prior year

Revenue Renewal
105%
prior year

New Customers
73
prior year

Customer Acquisition Cost
$151K
↑
prior year   +$10,652 vs. prior period

ACV per Customer
$154K
↑
prior year   +$4,520 vs. prior period

Customer Life Time Value
$880K
↑
prior year   +$132,251 vs. prior period

Customer Churn
1.67%
prior year

Revenue Churn
$75K
prior year   +$10,000 vs. prior period

Payback Period (in months)
11
prior year

CAC per $1 New ACV
$0.98
prior year   -$0.77 vs. prior period

▼ CMRR Trend
05/05/2015 10:39

$5,200,000
$3,900,000
$2,600,000
$1,300,000
$-1,300,000

Month Ending 11/30/2014 | Month Ending 12/31/2014 | Month Ending 01/31/2015 | Month Ending 02/28/2015 | Month Ending 03/31/2015 | Month Ending 04/30/2015 | Month Ending 05/31/2015

Add-on | Churn | New | Renewed

▼ Customer Trend
05/05/2015 10:39

160
120
80
40
0
-40

Month Ending 11/30/2014 | Month Ending 12/31/2014 | Month Ending 01/31/2015 | Month Ending 02/28/2015 | Month Ending 03/31/2015 | Month Ending 04/30/2015 | Month Ending 05/31/2015

Add-on | Churn | New | Renewed

▼ CAC Trend
05/05/2015 10:39

$7,000,000
$5,600,000
$4,200,000
$2,800,000
$1,400,000
$0

12/31/2012 | 12/31/2013 | 12/31/2014

Sales | Marketing

▼ CMRR Details
05/05/2015 10:39

CMRR	Year to Date 05/05/2015 Actual	Year Ending 12/31/2014 Actual
Beginning CMRR	$5,400,000	$4,235,000
New CMRR	172,062	940,000
Add-on	73,575	300,000
Churn	151,343	75,000
Ending CMRR	$5,494649,698	$5,400,00
Total # of Customers	375	368
Average CMRR per customer	$14,653	$14,674

▼ Churn Details
05/05/2015 10:39

	Year to Date 05/05/2015 Actual	Year Ending 12/31/2014 Actual	01/01/2015 Through 05/31/2015 Actual
Customers at the beginning of the year			
Customer Count	368	390	68
New Customers Added	10	73	(63)
Lost Customers	(3)	(5)	2
Total # of Customers	375	368	7
Customer Count			

▼ CAC Details
05/05/2015 10:39

	Actual	Test Budget	Budget	Budget % Var
Sales & Marketing				
Sales				
Plum On-Premise License	4,552,000	3,641,600	910,400	24.99
Plum On-Demand Subscription	2,000,000	2,600,000	(600,00)	(23.07)
Total Sales	6,552,000	6,241,600	310,400	4.97
Marketing				
Plum On-Premise License	1,000,000	800,000	200,000	24.99
Plum On-Demand Subscription	3,500,000	4,200,000	(700,00)	(16.66)
Total Marketing	4,500,000	5,000,000	(500,00)	(10.00)
Total Sales & Marketing	11,052,00	11,241,600	(189,600)	(1.68)

Figure 12.3 Executive Metrics Dashboard

Figure 12.3 shows an executive metrics dashboard available from the Intacct ERP application that can easily be shared in real time across the key stakeholders of your company to understand the financial impact of churn and retention on the velocity of your business.

In addition to conducting regular deep dives into the quantitative information regarding your churn and retention, the best practice is to also leverage an unbiased third party to conduct interviews with customers who churn so your company can better understand what happened and why. (Many excellent firms offer just such a service.) Leveraging a third-party service for this process will yield greater insight than having internal resources from your company conduct these post-churn interviews. Approach these in the same way your company would leverage a third-party service to conduct win/loss surveys for your new business.

The preceding discussion will deepen your understanding of churn and retention at a level that will help your company focus on the right priorities and accelerate growth. However, this does not come without an operational cost to the organization. An emerging best practice is to hire a customer success operations headcount. Customer success operations can help operationalize your company's customer success programs cross-functionally; it's not realistic to expect your customer-facing resources to have the bandwidth or the skill set to project-manage these programs successfully. In addition, customer success operations should help manage the underlying systems that help automate processes and provide the insight and visibility your company needs to keep customers for life.

Additional Commentary

You'd be crazy to run a business without deeply understanding the fundamentals of that business, right? That's no less true for any recurring revenue business that depends on maximizing retention and minimizing churn for long-term success. But, as with any business, there are levels of understanding and then there are *levels* of understanding. It's one thing to know that your installed base ARR went up by 8 percent (net retention of 108%) last year. It's a whole 'nother thing to know the details:

- What percentage of customers increased their contract size?
- Which industry had the highest churn rate?
- What are our retention and growth rates by product?

- By what average amount did we reduce discounts at first renewal?
- What is the average contract size versus original contract size of all customers who have been customers more than three years?

Knowing the details, not just at the high-level, but within each and every transaction, is a critical component of properly managing your business.

High Touch

This law is critical across all tiers and all touch models. The one advantage with customers in the high-touch model is that you can talk to them. For example, it's really important to understand why a customer churned when that happens. It's one thing to have a field in your CRM system that forces a CSM to pick from a drop-down list. That's a must for sure. But you will learn so much more by actually having a conversation with that customer. In life, we learn much more from our failures than from our successes, so we should take advantage of these failures and learn everything we can in order to avoid them in the future.

Low Touch

Following this law is mostly about financial mechanics. Can you track the details of every transaction in a granular way so you completely understand the nuances of your retention/churn or growth if you are purely pay-as-you-go. The one thing that is not purely financial mechanics is the *why*. Why did customer X churn? Why has customer Y grown by 243 percent in two years? You'll have some of these answers anecdotally within your company, and you'll have to weigh the value of having someone talk to some subset of them to get more information. You may also be able to find out more through a survey than you would otherwise, so that's worth considering.

Tech Touch

Again, you could identify some customers and talk to them but most likely you'll want to use some kind of digital methodology to learn what you can outside of the transactional specifics. Handpicking a subset of customers and providing an incentive for responding to a survey might be a useful tactic.

13 | Law 9: Drive Customer Success through Hard Metrics

Author: Jon Herstein, Senior Vice President of Customer Success, Box

Relevance

	LOW	MEDIUM	HIGH
B2B SaaS	★	★	★
SUBSCRIPTION	★	★	★
PAY-AS-YOU-GO	★	★	★
B2C	★	★	
TRADITIONAL	★	★	

Executive Summary

Customer success is still relatively new as a formal organization within the enterprise. As with any new business endeavor, maturity is required to ensure long-term viability. It's that time for customer success. Repeatability, process definition, measurement, and optimization are the hallmarks of that maturation. We see glimpses of these at more mature recurring revenue businesses, but there's still a long way to go for most.

Ultimately, the purpose of customer success, like any other part of a thriving company, is to achieve real business outcomes. Defining what success means both for you and for your customers, then establishing clear metrics that will deliver those business outcomes, is a necessary part of accelerating the maturation process. You can't improve what you don't measure.

In the late 1980s, Carnegie Mellon's Software Engineering Institute began to develop a process maturity framework that would help organizations improve their software process. Published several years later, the Capability Maturity Model for Software (CMM) became the go-to reference for assessing the process maturity of software development organizations. Equally important, the CMM framework has been used as a more generalized reference for determining how *mature* an organization—and its processes—has become, and serves as a guidebook for how to move from the *initial* level of maturity to the *optimizing* level.

Why is CMM relevant almost 30 years later in the (very different) world of customer success? Its basic premise is that, as organizations evolve their capabilities, they get progressively better and more predictable at executing their mission. This is true whether that mission is building great software or ensuring a consistently excellent customer experience. And the hallmarks of progression through the levels of maturity are repeatability, process definition, measurement, and optimization. Putting it all together, if we can measure and optimize the processes relevant to our customer success organizations, we are significantly more likely to reach our likely business objectives (high customer satisfaction, low churn, revenue expansion, etc.).

At Level 1 (initial), work gets done through the heroic actions of committed people without much regard for process or repeatability. Sound familiar? If you manage a handful of CSMs (or fewer), this is probably your daily reality. The objective your CSMs are focused on is along the lines of "Do whatever it takes to make your customers successful and make sure they renew!" The role of the CSM at this stage is likely to be poorly defined; details beyond this objective are left to individuals to figure out as they go. Assuming that you've got good people, this will actually work for a while. But your short-term gain (customer happiness) will likely result in long-term pain (overworked people, inconsistent delivery, uneven/inconsistent results).

Progressing to Level 2 (*repeatable*) occurs when the necessary process discipline is in place to repeat earlier successes. From there, achieving Level 3 maturity (*defined*) occurs when the process is documented, standardized, and integrated into a standard process for the organization. At this point, the fundamentals of a repeatable process methodology are in place, and what remains is measurement (Level 4: *managed*) and consistent improvement (Level 5: *optimizing*).

Assuming that your customer success organization has identified its repeatable processes and clearly defined and documented them, your focus will turn to active measurement and optimization. But what can and should be measured, and what are the benefits of doing so? Broadly speaking, you can think of three categories of metrics to explore: (1) customer behavior, (2) CSM activity, and (3) business outcomes. You will find a vast set of possible metrics within each of the buckets, and the following discussion will attempt to provide just a few relevant examples. Each business (and accompanying customer success organization) will need to determine which of these metrics matter and how, exactly, to define and measure them.

Customer and User Behavior

One of the biggest advantages of the SaaS delivery model for software, as compared to on-premise software, is that we can instrument and measure every aspect of how customers use our products. Previously, a software vendor had no practical way to determine whether or how the intended user base used its software. In properly instrumented SaaS applications, we are aware of every login, click, upload, download, error generated, and so forth. We know the frequency with which users perform specified activities. And depending on the nature of the product, we may also know the business value of these activities (e.g., a SaaS provider of an e-commerce platform will know the value of the transactions it has processed). The trick, of course, is correlating usage metrics to derived business value (for the customer) and how that will ultimately affect retention/expansion.

Examples of user-based metrics may include (but aren't limited to):

- NPS
- Logins and logouts
- Usage of specific product features/platforms (online, mobile, API)

If you are operating a B2B model, you may also aggregate user-level behavior (and other customer-level behavior, such as payments made) into a higher-level view of customer "health." This may include identifying risk factors that you have correlated to likelihood of churn, such as payment/nonpayment, engagement with the customer's administrator, and referenceability.

One important note of caution: The behavior of your customer's users serves only as a proxy for the business value the customer is deriving. To paraphrase Nick Mehta, Gainsight CEO, no one buys your software so they can log into it. Your customer has subscribed to your solution to fulfill one or more business objectives: find more leads, generate more revenue, make manufacturing more efficient, or enhance collaboration with suppliers. The key is to understand what those objectives are and how your product relates to them. In some cases, you won't be able to ensure your customer is meeting its intended objectives solely through the instrumentation built into your product. For example, if customers are using your file-sharing solution to eliminate FTP servers, you'll have to ask them whether they've actually done so; your product provides no visibility into this. Spend time with your customers at the beginning of the relationship to understand their business objectives and agree on how you will jointly measure the results.

Customer Success Manager Activity

Once you've defined the processes for your CSMs, it is natural to wonder how well those processes are being followed. From there, you will want to understand how the activities in which CSMs are engaging (or not engaging) affect customer sentiment and retention. Having a comprehensive understanding and proper measurement of these processes will lead to insights into the performance of your people, as well as into how much these activities actually matter to business outcomes. For example, are your QBRs as effective as you think they are in driving great adoption of your product? Do face-to-face visits outperform e-mail and phone calls when it comes to customer satisfaction?

Examples of CSM activity metrics may include:

- Frequency of various types of interactions with customers (QBRs, e-mail updates, phone calls)
- Support ticket volume handled by CSMs (rather than your support team)
- Timeliness of risk identification
- Effectiveness of risk mitigation efforts

Business Outcomes

An added benefit of maturation toward measurement and optimization is greater predictability of outcomes. Want to know how many customers a CSM can effectively manage (ideal account ratio)? Measure the relevant business outcomes for cohorts of CSMs with varied account loads. Interested in understanding how effective formal quarterly business reviews are vis-à-vis more frequent, informal check-ins? Measure customer engagement and satisfaction for cohorts that vary on this dimension.

Note that this section refers to the business outcomes that matter to you (retention, expansion, etc.). You must work with various functions within your organization (product, marketing, sales, finance) to determine what "success" looks like and which metrics indicate how you're doing. You'll be designing your processes, activities, and metrics around the definition of success and measuring accordingly. In many cases, you will share responsibility for success with the other groups: For example, customer success and product are jointly responsible for ensuring that users of your product adopt it. The more clarity you can drive around *ownership* of these metrics, the more you can refine the processes and behaviors your team will execute.

Examples of business outcome metrics may include:

- Gross retention
- Net retention
- Expansion
- Logo retention
- Customer satisfaction
- NPS

Clearly defining what success means, both to you and your customers, ensures greater clarity of your customer success team's mission and responsibility. Once you've achieved alignment on this definition, it's critical to articulate the things you will measure to demonstrate how the team is performing. These metrics enable customer success leaders to prove the value of the customer success organization and improve your contribution to the company's overall performance over time. Finally, your CSMs will thank you for the clarity of purpose this brings them, as well as the enhanced ability to truly understand their own performance and contributions.

Remember: you get what you measure! So figure out what matters, and then start defining and focusing on those key metrics.

Additional Commentary

This law is obviously directed at those who have actual customer success teams. If that's the case for you, it's absolutely necessary to actively manage your team with very specific metrics, just like you do your sales team or any other team. At some point, headcount needs to be justified by metrics, not by begging. If you are a volume B2B business or a B2C business, you will someday, if you don't already, have a customer success team. It might be only one or two people for thousands, or even millions, of customers, but someone will be responsible for the customer experience and will be measured on the key customer success metrics. The techniques of a team of CSMs who have some reasonable number of accounts each (5 to 150) will clearly be very different from those who are responsible for thousands or millions. We've explored that at some length with our discussion of high-touch, low-touch, and tech-touch models. At the highest level, the driving metrics are the same for all models, and they are basically the company-level metrics, too—retention, churn, upsell, and so on. If you are managing individuals with CSM responsibilities, you'll need to go deeper on their metrics. Retention, upsell, and churn are the right long-term metrics, but they are lagging metrics and not particularly predictive. More on that in the high-touch section that follows.

In the infancy stage of customer success, which we are still in, the measurements really have been akin to baby food. We've had hundreds, even thousands, of very fluffy, one-on-one conversations with our CSMs. We ask good questions wanting to help them, such as:

- How are your customers doing overall?
- Are there any customers at risk of churn?
- You've been working with customer X on some challenges for the past 60 days, are we making progress?
- Customer Y churned. What could we have done differently?
- How can I help?

These are all reasonable questions to ask someone responsible for the retention and overall success of a particular book of business, but none of them are very measurable. This is again a place where a customer success management solution can be extremely helpful. They have the ability to change your one-on-ones so they sound more like this:

- Your average health score across all your customers is six points lower than the rest of the team. It looks like the component that is dragging you down is the executive relationship. Let's put together a plan to change that, starting with the lowest-scoring customer.
- You have three at-risk customers up for renewal in the next 90 days. Let's review your action plan for each of those customers.
- Your upsell rates are 10 percent higher than the next-best CSM. That's awesome, and I'd like you to put together three slides we can review and you can share at our next team meeting to help everyone else step up their game to your level.

It's not hard to figure out which one of those one-on-ones is more effective for both the manager and the employee. As with all disciplines, active management is possible only if there are clear measurables. This allows you to manage the results but coach the process. It's imperative, as the discipline of customer success matures, that the ability to effectively manage the team and the individuals evolves as well and is based on specific measurables that drive bottom-line business value.

High Touch

Managing and measuring customer success people in a high-touch model is very similar to managing sales reps. For a sales rep, there's only one metric that really matters, right? How much did you sell? At some point, that's the lone measurement that determines success or failure. But, does a good sales VP wait 12 months, or even a quarter, to see what a sales rep's results are to determine whether they are good? Of course not. There are lots of things they'll be looking at along the way that they believe are indicators of future success. Some of the more measurable ones are

- Pipeline size
- Pipeline growth
- Pipeline movement
- Number of calls
- Number of meetings
- Number of proposals created and sent
- Average forecasted deal size

And there are many more. Of course there are also a bunch of more subjective things that will be observed and coached, too, such as skill at delivering the standard sales pitch, ability to overcome objections, and so on. Every job has some highly measurable aspects and some less tangible elements, too.

Customer success is no different. I'll argue that the key metric to determine the quality of an individual CSM or the whole team is net retention. This takes into account both retention and upsell. I've said this before and I'll say it again. Successful customers do two things: (1) They stay with you as a customer (renew their contracts if on a subscription). (2) They buy more stuff from you. If customer success's job is to make customers successful and that's what successful customers do, then net retention is the metric that matters for them. However, just as with sales reps, you probably don't want to wait for 12 months to see the net retention number for a CSM's entire book of business. You'll want to measure the elements that help you predict whether the CSM is successful far in advance of a renewal or upsell event. Much like a CRM system does for sales, a customer success management solution can do this for customer success. You can also track many of these manually if you don't have a CSM solution:

- Health score across book of business
- Health score trends
- Level of direct CSM engagement

- Number of triggered actions (low survey score, no product usage)
- Number of triggered actions completed
- Number of upsell opportunities identified
- Number of positive relationship activities (references, case studies, etc.)

And, of course, there are subjective things to watch, too, such as their depth of product knowledge, ability to utilize other resources wisely, and many more.

The bottom line is that there's no excuse for fluffy one-on-ones any longer with high-touch customer success teams. We need to rapidly move into highly measurable, highly actionable metrics that help the individuals to improve and drive positive company results.

Low Touch

Everything we said with regard to the high-touch model is true here in the low-touch model, too. The same challenges and opportunities exist to start measuring the things that matter with regard to building an effective team or program and, more importantly, having a positive impact on your customers.

In many ways, this is more critical the lower touch your model is, because you can't rely on relationships to win the day or understand the customer. If I'm a high-touch CSM with five clients, I can tell you with a great deal of accuracy the health score for each of my customers. I just know because I talk to them all the time. If I have 200 customers and I'm forced to operate with a much lower touch, I will be much more dependent on any kind of metrics that can be automatically reported about my customers. In this environment, it becomes almost imperative to have a CSM solution, but many of the following could be tracked manually if an automated solution is not available. The list below is an extension of the list we started earlier in the high-touch section:

- Survey scores (this is often incorporated into the health score but can be tracked separately, especially if you haven't developed a health score yet)
- E-mail engagement (what do customers do with e-mails that come directly from you or from your marketing team?)

- Number of support tickets opened (this may not be a good measurement of a customer success individual or team as it's probably out of their control, but it can shine the light on troubled customers)
- Invoices—happy customers tend to pay their bills on time

Because you're ultimately measuring your customer success team on how well their customers are doing, anything that helps you understand that about your customers is an indicator (to varying degrees) of the success of the individuals responsible for those customers. It's not feasible to track everything, but track what you can so you have a temperature on your customers and some insight into how your team is doing.

Tech Touch

The great news about the tech-touch environment is that there are volumes of customers, which makes experimentation easier. In this model in which virtually all of your interactions with customers are technology driven, with e-mail being a primary vehicle, you can easily do some A/B testing to determine what works best. Let's say that you have an intervention scheduled for every customer when they reach an annual anniversary as a customer of yours. You could construct an e-mail with the exact same content but two different subject lines, one that says, "Congratulations" and another that says "Happy Birthday." And then you just watch the open/bounce/unsubscribe rates to see which was more effective.

In many ways, the tech-touch customer success team operates much like a marketing team whose interactions are primarily digital, too (website, e-mail, webinars, etc.). This leads to the conclusion that they can be measured in similar ways. That's essentially true. Much like marketing, your tech-touch customer success team should be measured on the effectiveness of their touches. That means measuring things such as:

- E-mail engagement
- Webinar attendance
- Community engagement
- User group participation

For marketing teams, the ultimate measure of their success is leads created (i.e., pipeline). For customer success teams, the ultimate measure is health score. It's not a coincidence that customer health score for customer success teams is analogous to pipeline for sales teams. Simply put, a sales pipeline is a predictor of future behavior, such as likelihood of closing, timing of closing, deal size, and so on. The pipeline is the primary input to a sales VP's forecast. Health score for a customer success VP provides the same insights. An accurate health score is a great predictor of future customer behavior, such as likelihood of retention, possibility of upsell, level of risk, and so on. In the end, everything your customer success team does should be designed to create loyalty, and loyalty is measured in the long term by net retention and in the short term by health score.

The discipline of customer success is changing rapidly, like a child going through a growth spurt. One of the areas of most rapid change is in the measurement and management of our customers and, by extension, the teams that are responsible for those customers. To become an adult with a seat at the big table, this trend needs to continue so that CFOs and CEOs can see the fruits of their investments.

14 | Law 10: It's a Top-Down, Company-Wide Commitment

Author: Nick Mehta, Chief Executive Officer, Gainsight

Relevance

	LOW	MEDIUM	HIGH
B2B SaaS	★	★	★
SUBSCRIPTION	★	★	★
PAY-AS-YOU-GO	★	★	★
B2C	★	★	★
TRADITIONAL	★	★	★

Executive Summary

Customer success is not just a department or an organization. It's a philosophy that must pervade your entire company. For most of business history, only two things have really mattered: (1) building the product and (2) selling the product. We believe that the time has come for a third core process to emerge—customer success.

Customer success is not just the buzz phrase du jour. It's here and it's here to stay. Done well, customer success drives real value to the bottom line of your business. If you are not on board yet, you will be soon because you can't survive without it. Luckily, getting started is not that difficult. But customer success starts at the top, and it must be a company-wide commitment.

Customer success. It sounds like a truism that says nothing new or interesting. After years of hearing CEOs say customers are king and watching them do the opposite, it's easy to be cynical about the new customer success movement.

In this law, I hope to convince you about the following four points:

1. What customer success is (for real)
2. Why customer success is inevitable
3. How customer success drives value
4. Where to start

What Customer Success Is (for Real)

As many B2B companies create teams with labels such as *customer success management* or *chief customer officer*, you might think *customer success* is a department.

But just as sales is both a team and a cross-functional activity, customer success is a company-wide matter. Literally, customer success involves shifting the orientation of your company from your product or your sales to your customers' success.

For most of business history, companies have focused on two core processes: (1) building product and (2) selling product. In the customer success movement, we argue for a third core process: driving customer success. Put simply, if you bet on delivering success for your customers, then success for your business (in terms of sales and profits) will follow. This is a big bet, and it takes support across customer success, finance, marketing, sales, and product teams, hence, the company-wide commitment. And if you're a CEO or a senior executive, you set the tone for this commitment.

In the customer success movement, all business questions are reframed around the customer's success:

- **Product:** Which feature will truly help our clients achieve their goals using our solution (versus being demoware)?
- **Sales:** Which clients are likely to be good fits for our solution (versus ones that will leave us quickly)?
- **Marketing:** What messages authentically align with the success and value we deliver (versus being buzzwords)?
- **Finance:** Which metrics reflect real success and value for our clients (versus just new sales)?

Why Customer Success Is Inevitable

The good news is that you don't need to think too hard about the *if* here. Customer success is a natural outcome of massive changes in the economy:

- Globalization and technology have dropped the barrier to entry for businesses.
- Lowered barrier to entry allows new entrants to disrupt almost every established category.
- New entrants have created lower-friction business models.
- Lower-friction business models make it easy for customers to try and buy—with shorter-term pricing (monthly or yearly); granular consumption (per minute, per CPU cycle, per user, per click); and easier deployment (cloud and mobile).
- At the same time, this lower friction makes it easier for customers who *try* and *buy* to say *bye* and leave.
- At the end of the day, customers have the power and customers have choice.
- Customers with choice will choose to stay with vendors that deliver the outcomes and success they desire.
- Indeed, customers will start *expecting* vendors to focus on success as more of them do so and as the applications for consumers (e.g., Uber) do such a great job at this.

It's not a matter of whether it will happen. The question is will your business react quickly enough to survive when it does happen?

How Customer Success Drives Value

On the positive side, companies that embrace this opportunity early will achieve massive results by focusing on customer success:

- **Growth:** Facing less headwind in the form of churn and more tailwind in the form of upsell, businesses that focus on customer success simply grow faster. And successful customers become advocates and references to drive more new clients. In the long run, the *leaky bucket* effect of churn cannot be counteracted by new business alone.
- **Valuation:** According to an Altimeter Capital report *Valuation of Subscription Businesses* (October 2014), public subscription business multiples are directly correlated to customer success and retention: "Dollar renewal rate (DRR) is the most important metric for valuing subscription businesses." In short, Wall Street notices customer success.
- **Differentiation:** Finally, because not every company in every category is focused on customer success, customer success management can become a meaningful differentiator. Customers know that products and services become commoditized over time. The business process and team a company uses to drive success for its clients is really what matters in the long run. The sales messaging of best-in-class companies talks about the customer success process in a meaningful way.

Where to Start

If you're convinced, you're probably thinking, "How the heck do I implement a 'top-down, company-wide commitment'? Where do I start?" Here are a few ideas:

- **Define success:** One of the biggest steps you can take to create a customer success–centric culture is to crystallize what success means for your customers. Many companies sell horizontal products that can be used in a variety of use cases. If you're a CEO or a senior executive, you should kick off a cross-functional process to canonize the common use cases for your offering and define what success would mean to the customer in each of those use cases. Here's a simple way to think about this: If you asked customers, "What does wild success with our company mean to you?" what would they say? Without defining the goal, it's hard to get the company rallied around it.

- **Align around success:** Next, review your organization and make sure that each functional area knows what it must do to support customer success. Your customer success team can be the quarterback of the initiative, but it needs buy-in from each department. This could mean:
  - Reviewing customer success feedback each month with the product team
  - Defining and refining sales qualification criteria
  - Reviewing messaging regularly with the marketing and customer success teams
- **Listen to the customer success team:** If you're a senior executive or a CEO, you are likely flooded with signals about your business—from customers, partners, investors, and employees. You need to make sure a key part of that signal comes from the customer success team or are informed by the results of your customer success practices if you don't yet have a team, since they are the eyes and ears of your customer base. Establish a regular review of customer success issues. Include a customer success executive in every executive meeting, every board meeting, and every key strategic decision. And take his or her opinions as seriously as you take those of your sales leader.
- **Prioritize customer success:** This is where the rubber meets the road. Every business has limited resources and must make trade-offs. Is the feature to delight clients always getting deprioritized for the feature to drive demos? Is the project to implement self-service getting pushed behind the channel partner rollout? Is the training for CSMs being postponed for the sales training? If you want to drive customer success, prioritize it.
- **Empower the customer success team:** In the same vein, if you've created a team to drive success with your customers, take measures to support it. Some things to consider:
  - Make sure the title for the customer success executive is on par with the sales leader.
  - Keep your CSM in the loop when a customer escalates to the management team.
  - Let the CSM be the hero with customers if possible (e.g., ideally the CSM will tell the customer that you agreed to their contract change or road map request).
  - Make it clear to the rest of the organization that the CSM represents the client's views.
- **Measure customer success:** Customer success will never be taken seriously if there aren't agreed-upon metrics to apply. Define metrics for your bottom-line results, including gross churn, net retention, and

other measures. Make sure everyone is clear on what the metrics mean. And create some early-warning metrics such as health score, adoption score, and NPS to track where customer success is going.

- **Report on customer success:** Next, make these metrics very visible. Show them in your all-hands meetings. Display them on your walls and monitors. Spend as much time on customer success in your board meetings as you do on sales. Create a killer customer success section of your board packet to show your board that you take it seriously.
- **Incent toward customer success:** Companies set compensation plans to drive behavior. So if you want to drive customer success, pay people for it. Consider adding customer success metrics (e.g., net retention, NPS, or health score) to your company bonus plan.
- **Challenge the company:** Just as you push the company to grow sales and hit quarterly targets, expend as much effort pushing the company to hit customer success targets, such as retention, go-lives, satisfaction metrics, or adoption goals.
- **Celebrate success:** Customer success isn't easy. It's not always in your control, and customers can be challenging. Most companies have great traditions for cheering sales on—gongs, champagne, trips, fun bets. Do the same for customer success. Get yourself a CSM gong and send the signal that customer success is a top-down, company-wide commitment.

Additional Commentary

It's hard to overstate the value of this law for companies that are serious about customer success. In some ways, it's not just another law on a list of 10 but perhaps the stone tablets the laws are written on. This is literally the foundation for all the other laws. More than any other organization in an enterprise, customer success needs the commitment of every other organization. I said *commitment*, not *help*. Help will be necessary at times, too, but that word implies that it's an anomaly and can be considered only when a specific scenario arises. That's just not true. A real commitment to customer success begins before the first marketing foray is aimed at the first prospect, before the first line of code is written in the product, and before the first sales call happens. That's the nature of the Ten Laws in aggregate, articulating what great recurring revenue businesses need to think about and do well *across the company* in order to actually *be* great. This isn't an afterthought or an organization that picks up the pieces when things go wrong. It's a philosophy that starts at the top and permeates the entire company and then, and only then, can it become an organization that participates alongside all other organizations to ensure that the company's focus is on driving business success *for the customer* first and foremost.

None of this can happen unless your CEO is fully committed, and a CEO cannot be fully committed to anything unless his board is equally bought in. One of the pleasant realities of the customer success movement is that investors are more and more interested in the associated outcomes—high retention, increased upsell, improved customer satisfaction—and are pushing earlier investment in customer success as an integral part of building a viable company. This great news comes with a cost of course: The need to be smart about those investments, both in technology and in people. One more reason this has to start at the top.

The list of ways that your CEO drives customer success is really long, but the last one I'll mention here is about culture. Because great companies will have customer success in their DNA, it needs to become part of your culture. And, as you all know, culture may be managed and nurtured by your human resources team, but it's established, reinforced, and modeled primarily by the boss. Making customer success a part of your culture is often harder for more mature companies because it may be a dramatic shift from the way the company was built. Changes such as that need to come down from the top and be part of the company's rewards and incentives programs. One of the best examples I've seen came from a very successful, now public, SaaS company in which the executive bonus plan made it clear what the CEO's priorities were. Quarterly executive bonuses were paid based on only two criteria: (1) new business bookings and (2) renewal rate. To fund the plan above $0 required a minimum threshold to be reached on both metrics. The message this sent is clear: retention rates are just as important to our business as new customer acquisition.

As we explored in Chapter 2, the impact of customer success needs to be felt in sales and marketing, product management and development, and services. Each of these, along with the customer success organization itself, is an equal-strength link in the chain. The tension created by the constant focus on existing customers that is brought by your customer success leadership and your CEO will drive the company forward in a positive way. Oversight, direction, and commitment from the top are invaluable in creating the right balance. Think through these five questions as a CEO (if you are one) or about your CEO (if you're not). Ask whether your CEO is truly focused on customer success:

1. Is he willing to say "no" to an above-ASP deal in your pipeline because the chances of making the customer truly successful are too small?
2. Is he willing to delay a vital product release in order to address current customer challenges?
3. Is the head of customer success in his circle of trust?
4. Does your road map include things that won't help you sell more but only address existing customer needs?
5. Does he get personally involved in critical customer situations as often as he does in key sales deals?

I've obviously painted each of these as black and white although business decisions often happen in shades of gray. But forcing a yes or no, even theoretically, can often bring truth to light. If your answer to each as a CEO is not a quick *yes*, then you need to consider whether you are truly focused on customer success. If you are a non-CEO executive and aren't sure whether the answer to each question is *yes* for your CEO, then you should consider carefully what that means to you and to your company. I'm not saying that you are doomed to failure because you're not sure how he would answer one question, but it's worthwhile to think about what that means and how it might affect you.

High Touch, Low Touch, and Tech Touch

This law does not vary in any way based on the model or models through which you deal with your customers. Success in every case is highly dependent on the commitment of your board and CEO and the alignment of customer success with the other organizations in your company. There may be, however, some variation in the trade-offs that need to be considered within each model:

- High Touch: hiring another CSM to manage some of your most critical customers versus hiring another quota-carrying sales rep.
- Low Touch: driving incremental bookings by decreasing CSM's book of business versus increasing sales quotas.
- Tech Touch: building a customer portal vs upgrading your marketing automation solution.

Each of those trade-offs is about an increased investment in customer success versus investing in another organization. I'm not saying that the right answer is always about customer success. My goal is simply to point out that tough investment decisions will need to be made regardless of the touch model(s) you are employing and that your CEO is likely to be involved in many of them. A focus and long-term commitment to customer success will show itself over the course of the hundreds of decisions a company has to make every month.

An instructive story on this theme was shared with me recently by Jim Steele. Jim spent 13 years at Salesforce on the executive staff as the chief customer officer and president of worldwide sales. The night before the first Dreamforce customer conference in 2003, the executive team gathered with Marc Benioff to review the agenda and run through all the presentations. As with most conferences held by software vendors, the agenda was filled with product presentations designed to highlight the features and value of the Salesforce platform. About halfway through the review, Benioff made an executive decision that set the tone for the entire company for years to come. He decided to throw out all of the product presentations in favor of creating an open microphone opportunity for customers to share direct feedback. Instead of telling their customers how great they were, Benioff opted for having the customers speak their mind while Salesforce listened. Not only that, but when each customer took his or her turn at the microphone, he specifically requested feedback on what was wrong with the Salesforce product, with their processes, or with their people. No customer got away with simply singing their praises.

I was not there, but I'm guessing this was not an easy decision and was based on Benioff's principle of putting the customer first. In retrospect, it may seem like a no-brainer, but, at the time, with all sorts of time and effort having been poured into the product presentations, I'm sure it didn't go over quite so well nor did it come without risk. But the impact on the customers was no doubt profound and, on Salesforce itself, perhaps even more profound. Putting customers first sounds good but isn't always an easy decision. That's why it needs to become part of the culture and the corporate DNA so that each situation is not so much a decision as *just the way we do things*.

Chief Customer Officer, Technology, and Future

15

The Rise of the Chief Customer Officer

When organizations change, and especially when new ones appear, new titles tend to come along for the ride. Shortly after IT took its place of prominence in the enterprise, the title CIO started to become popular as well. Today, it's the norm. Any decent-sized company has a CIO. No one questions whether it's necessary or whether there's enough responsibility to justify the *C*. It's a given when you consider the technology dependence of virtually every company in the world and especially when you consider the liability involved in the protection of a company's key information. The existence of the cloud has only served to up the ante as it's become part of every company's IT infrastructure and the home of volumes of business-critical data. There's no doubt that CIOs are here to stay.

Time will tell if the same is true for the new title that's becoming part of the customer success landscape—chief customer officer (CCO). For all the reasons we've outlined earlier, customer success is certainly here to stay and most likely the same is true for the CCO title. But what does that title actually mean? What are the typical responsibilities? Why did it take the customer success movement to make it prominent? Let's explore.

Wikipedia defines *chief customer officer* this way: "A chief customer officer (CCO) is the executive responsible in customer-centric companies for the total relationship with an organization's customers."

The *Before Cloud* Chief Customer Officer

That's a pretty good definition, and, as you can see, a position with that responsibility would logically align with virtually any company in the world. Thus, it's not a new position/title, but it was seen pretty sparingly up until recently when the subscription tsunami raised the visibility and importance of customers to a whole new level. In the world BC (before cloud), the CCO role appeared primarily at companies that used it, in part, to make a public statement about how important customers were to them. One executive whose entire responsibility it was to make the customer's journey and experience better—sounds like a really good idea, right? And, if done well and supported 100 percent from the top, it was better than a good idea; it was a great idea.

But the challenges were many to making a measurable impact. The primary obstacle was that the CCO in the pre-subscription days seldom had any direct operational responsibility and, therefore, no bottom-line revenue or profitability metrics for which they were accountable. That's not to say that their efforts were not positive and significant, just really hard to quantify.

Let's play out an oversimplified example. The focus of the CCO in the pre-subscription days was usually defined around *the customer experience*, often referred to as CX. Most companies truly want to be easy to do business with. They want all customer touch points to be frictionless and leave a positive impression on the customer. One of the touch points for every customer is the vendor's invoicing process. Depending on the complexity of your product, invoices can range from simple to nightmarish. Look at your own cell phone bill for a good example of nightmarish. And then think about how much time and effort AT&T spends explaining invoices to customers. Lots. A CCO with overall customer experience responsibility might very well seize on the invoicing process as a source of irritation for customers and seek to improve it. For larger companies, this will be an enormous undertaking. Making all invoices accurate, simple, and timely is an extremely positive thing for customers. No one could possibly dispute that. But the effort involved will be significant and, certainly painful, and will result in what? A better experience for the customer? Absolutely. More revenue for the company? Maybe but hard to quantify. An increase in profitability? Probably not but, again, very hard to measure. Existing customers spending more money with you? Could be, but how could you ever prove that?

So you see the challenges. I know many who have performed this role back in the *good old days* and with great satisfaction, knowing that their efforts really did change the customers' experience and improved how their company was viewed and trusted by their customers. But it was constantly frustrating to be working so hard and doing so much good and not being able to specifically tie it to the things the CEO was measured on by the board. The result was that funding that expensive position was a risk and an expense most CEOs were not willing to take. Now you could accuse them of not being customer-centric, but we all work for someone, and, if the board is holding a CEO accountable for revenue, profitability, product quality, and market share, and a CCO can't tie her accomplishments to any of those things, the choice to not add that position to the executive staff is pretty understandable.

To all of our benefit, CX has found its way into thousands of companies and changed the way they interact with their customers. But it's pretty rare for that discipline to have become important enough to generate a CCO title. As we mentioned in Chapter 2, CX and customer success are two parts of the same jigsaw puzzle and are overlapping in at least one significant way—surveys as a provider of insights and customer feedback.

For the most part (but not exclusively), CX measures itself by customer satisfaction surveys. In the previous example regarding invoicing, the project may very well start with a survey that asks customers about their satisfaction with the vendor's invoicing process and perhaps even drill in on the key elements—accuracy, simplicity, and timeliness. That becomes the baseline for the project and then a post-project survey with the same questions is done, and the results are compared to quantify the benefits and justify the effort. It's a perfectly reasonable way to determine the validity of the undertaking. The overlap between CX and customer success occurs because customer success will also use surveys to help understand customer health (Customer Success Law 4). They are not the whole story, but direct feedback from customers is certainly part of the overall picture of customer health and will help customer success teams prioritize customer interactions. Because the goals are really the same for both groups—improved customer health and customer experience leading to increased loyalty—they are likely to start coming together organizationally.

In the days BC, and even to this day in non-subscription companies, the CCO role has been thought of primarily as a marketing job and even as a replacement for the chief marketing officer title. Not coincidentally, CX usually lives in marketing as well. Both of these are signals of another positive trend brought on largely by the power of information and its fingertip availability to anyone and everyone. Generally speaking, many marketing organizations are moving to anchor themselves to the bottom line of the company and engaging customers, not just selling to them, is their means to that end. Today's customers, empowered by their access to information, can't simply be seen as buyers. They want to be listened to, engaged with, and basically treated as partners. This becomes a noble goal for a VP of marketing, a CMO, or a CCO and provides tremendous benefits to the rest of the company thirsty for more insights and understanding about their customers. In the absence of other organizations thinking strategically about customers, marketing rightly picked up the ball and ran with it. Customer support and services, with their thousands of daily interactions with customers, had a similar opportunity, but the tactical focus required for their daily success on fixing customer problems and completing services projects worked against them becoming as strategic or long-term focused as the business required.

And that was the state of the world up until sometime around the turn of the millennium when subscriptions and cloud and SaaS and social media thundered into our consciousness.

The New Chief Customer Officer

I've seen customer success organizations grow up inside almost every organization in the enterprise. It's very common inside sales because the sales VP is often the person, at least early on at a subscription company, who owns the renewal process and the renewal quota. Also very common is that customer success takes shape within the broader services organization because the initial focus and efforts of the customer success team tend to look a lot like some combination of consulting and support and require many of the same skills. For all the reasons described above, marketing is also a relatively common home, although much less so than sales or services. Last, I've seen it arise as part of the product team. The logic here is pretty clear, too. The product must be built to solve customer needs, and nobody will know more about the needs of customers than CSMs. But, as you have likely observed in your career, especially at smaller companies, organizations are often built around individuals, not simply on convention. But over time, consensus tends to form and some sort of best practice usually starts to emerge. For customer success, that trend is toward services.

I say *toward services* very carefully as opposed to *in services*. The reason that the movement is toward services is pretty simple. Customer success is rightly seen as a post-sales role, because the preponderance of effort and involvement happens after the prospect has become a customer. However, because we're on the subject, one of the many nuances in a subscription economy is that there's really no such thing as post-sales. Once the initial sale is complete, all effort is then applied to ensure the next sale, whether that's a renewal, a non-opt-out, or an upsell. It's fair to say that, in the subscription or pay-as-you-go economy, every single activity is a pre-sales activity. But, back to the subject at hand, the phrase *post-sales* is not going away, and it's well understood that it means "after the original sale" and that's where customer success belongs.

The post-sales organization tends to be pretty mature because the primary parts of it have been a necessary staple of the enterprise for a long time:

- Professional services
- Training
- Customer support
- Implementation/onboarding

Even CEOs have a breaking point with regard to how many direct reports they can effectively manage, so the post-sales organization tends to become consolidated over time. That usually means that a senior vice president (SVP) of services is hired or promoted internally to manage all of the above departments. It's more and more common that customer success becomes another department in that larger services organization, and, as we elaborated on in Chapter 2, the entire services organization often then takes on the umbrella term *customer success* as its moniker.

But what happens when the leader of the entire organization, once called the SVP of services, changes the name of the organization and, therefore, his title, and becomes the SVP of customer success? Nothing wrong with that except the confusion caused by the department within the organization also called Customer Success, which may well also have a VP leading it. This can result in a bit of a *who's on first* routine in describing the overall organization. That's certainly not the best reason in the world to change someone's title to CCO, but it's definitely *a* reason. And if you combine that with the ownership of the overall retention number for the company, which will come with the addition of the customer success function, you can start building a pretty compelling case for adding this role to the C-suite.

At this point, we've described the morphing of the post-sales organization from what's seen in Figure 15.1 to what's in Figure 15.2.

For those who haven't encountered this type of organization, it's not at all like an SVP of sales overseeing four different sales groups:

1. Enterprise
2. Midmarket
3. SMB
4. Channel

Figure 15.1   The Old Post-Sales Organization

Figure 15.2   The New Post-Sales Organization

No one is saying that's an easy job by any means. But the primary focus and measurement of each of those four groups is identical—selling your product. The SVP of services (or CCO) has five groups in the organization described above by the second chart. But it's not about having more departments or more people. It's all about the breadth of responsibility as defined by the types of activities performed and the associated measurements. As you'll see in a moment, each one of these groups is separate and distinct in what they do, how they do it, and how they are measured. This is another factor in assessing whether the word *chief* is the first word in the title of this leader.

Professional Services

Primary Measurement—Utilization

Almost every software company, and many other companies, too, will have a professional services or consulting arm. This organization will be made up of people with very deep product and/or domain expertise that is applied, for a fee, on behalf of customers. This could be a consultant who has deep knowledge about how to use the Oracle invoicing product in a productive way. Or it could be the plumber who comes to your door and fixes your leaky sink. Neither one of them is trying to sell you either the software or the sink. They are selling you their expertise. In a nutshell, that's what we often call professional services or consulting.

The primary measurement for success in this business is called *utilization*. That basically means this: out of all of the hours available to be billed, how many hours were billed? If the plumber works 40 hours a week, he's going to be more profitable (and richer) if he can bill 30 of those hours than if he bills only 20. His primary task, assuming he has more work than he can handle, is to minimize his nonbillable hours and maximize his billable ones. The same is true for every consultant. And for the person who manages the professional services organization (and his bosses), that will be the number she looks at daily and for which she's held accountable.

Training

Primary Measurement—Number of Products Delivered

Everyone knows what training is so we won't reiterate that. Over the years, what's changed is the delivery mechanism. Classroom training is still done in the right situations, but, more and more, virtual training is becoming the norm, and on-demand is now a must-have as well. Not surprisingly, there are lots of technology options to help you execute on whatever channels you choose to use.

The key here again is to point out how different the roles are within this function and how the group as a whole should be measured. Training is run essentially as a product development team. Requirements are gathered, the product is built, and then the product is manufactured, sold, and delivered. The viability of the group rests on two things—quality of the product (does the student learn what they were intended to learn in a positive way?) and the number of products sold. Not all training organizations are designed to make money but as a company matures, training often becomes a source of revenue. Whether it generates dollars or not, "# of products delivered" is probably the right measurement for a training team. Alternatively, you could measure this from the customer's viewpoint and use a metric like "# of customers/users trained". In either case, it's very different from the way professional services is managed and measured.

Customer Support

Primary Measurement—Efficiency

Customer support is the break/fix organization. It's the team of people who take the calls or e-mails from customers who feel like something in the product is broken and who have come to expect some reasonable level of responsiveness, depending on the severity of the problem. In the software world customer support is the team of people who reactively assist customers with problems. Early on, the communication channel was primarily telephone, thus the euphemism "call center." But today this is often an organization interacting with customers via e-mail and chat as well as phone. Social media has also become part of the picture with some customer support teams taking cases from customers via Twitter, too.

Customer support is often seen as that necessary evil that exists only because of the impossibility of shipping perfect products. There are call centers around the world to help you put the crib together that you just bought for your newborn baby, to get you set up on an international calling plan for your upcoming trip to Europe, or to help you work around the bug you just discovered in trying to run that report.

In all of these situations, customer support is a cost center, and it will likely always be that way. It will also be, for the most part, a reactive organization. That's not a bad thing or a good thing, just a fact. And the way that you measure a cost center is by efficiency metrics like "*number of tickets closed per day per rep*" or "*total number of calls handled,*" metrics that tell you whether you're squeezing the most out of your investment. Typically, standard customer support is not something that is paid for separately by the customer so minimizing the cost per customer of providing that support will be high on the priority list for CFOs and those leading support teams. It's all about efficiency.

Implementation or Onboarding

Primary Measurement—Time-to-Value

As we discussed in depth in Chapter 11, your onboarding or implementation team is one of the key drivers of time-to-value in your company. No value can be derived from your product unless this is first done, and done well. It's not uncommon for the onboarding team to sit in the same group as your professional services team because the skills can be almost interchangeable. But, over time, most companies break these two groups apart for two reasons:

1. Measuring and improving timeliness of project completion in onboarding is so critical.
2. Packaging onboarding services is much more likely than professional services in which most work will be done on an hourly basis (time and materials).

Because onboarding services are almost always part of the initial sales deal, they are often packaged with fixed prices to make them easier to sell and to not slow down the sales cycle. Time-to-project-completion or time-to-value are the key metrics to drive improvement (and profitability) of your onboarding packages. Breaking this team out as a separate group allows you to start tracking the improvement of those metrics as the key determination of the effectiveness of this team. Ultimately, you could argue it's just another way to say utilization or efficiency but most would agree that timely and high-quality onboarding is so critical to the success and retention of customers that it requires its own group and measurement.

Customer Success

Primary Measurement—Retention

Customer success, as we've examined exhaustively, is a completely different organization from the others outlined previously. In some ways, it's the group that glues the other groups together. Customers have questions that go beyond what customer support can provide. They land in customer success. Customers need some consulting expertise in order to justify renewing their contract but not enough to justify an engagement. They land in customer success. Customers took training and went through onboarding but need just a little nudge here and a tweak there to reinforce those experiences. They land in customer success. And, at the same time, customer success, as the place where the buck stops (retention), pushes back on the other organizations to be better and faster at what they do. It really is a virtuous cycle from which the customer benefits greatly.

The goal and measurement is retention, net retention, renewal rate, or something along those lines. You could lump it all under the word *loyalty*. Customer success, whether high touch, low touch, or tech touch, is designed to build customer loyalty because loyal customers stay with their existing vendors and buy more stuff from them. It's as simple as that.

So that's five different organizations doing five very different things and being measured in five very different ways. That breadth of responsibility takes enormous intelligence, skill, and experience to manage and lead. I would argue that the skills and responsibilities of this role make it at least equivalent to that of a chief revenue officer who manages both

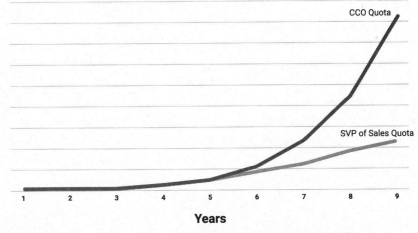

Figure 15.3   Quota Comparison—Sales versus CCO (Moderate to High-Growth Recurring Revenue Business)

marketing and sales. In fact, those two roles should be peers and have equivalent authority within the company. We've touched on this previously, but it's worth repeating that, in a maturing subscription or pay-as-you-go company, the revenue/bookings coming from existing customers greatly exceeds that coming from new customers. Figure 15.3 shows how those numbers diverge over time at a moderate-to-high-growth SaaS company.

This discussion so far explains the rise of the CCO and provides justification for that title if justification is required. But that's not even the end of the story. Much like software began to eat the world, customer success is kind of eating the enterprise. It's not hard to understand why. As your existing customer base becomes more and more valuable, the people responsible for nurturing and growing it become more valuable, too. Customer success has become a vortex sucking parts of other organizations into it as well. It's not a thirst for power; it's an acknowledgment of the shift in power happening in many companies across multiple industries. Another artifact of the subscription economy.

There are three other organizations, or parts of organizations, that are feeling the pull toward customer success and accelerating the rise of the CCO. The results will be different for different companies, but there are only two possibilities for these organizations as part of a customer success-centric enterprise: influence or absorption. Let's look at all three carefully to understand what is happening and why.

Sales

I made the comment earlier that, in a subscription or pay-as-you-go business, there's no such thing as post-sales. Every activity is a pre-sales activity. Simply put, that's because there's always another sale lurking whether it's a physical renewal or an opportunity for the customer to opt-out or an upsell of some kind. The selling process never ends, it just changes uniforms. Given that truth and the reality that most CEOs will want one person to be responsible for net retention (renewals and upsells), there's a logical argument for adding a sales function into the customer success organization for a number of reasons:

1. So CSMs can maintain their trusted adviser status uncompromised by negotiating sales deals of any kind.
2. So the CEO has *one throat to choke* when it comes to maintaining and growing the value of the customer base.
3. Because the CSM will have her finger on the pulse of any customer coming up for renewal and can help prep the sales rep with the history and background necessary for the renewal conversation.
4. Because the CSMs will be the best source of upsell leads for the sales rep and will help prep him for the opportunity.

In short, the person responsible for the net retention number, regardless of title, will have every right to ask for the resources required to deliver that number, including the quota-carrying sales rep(s) who are closing those deals. In addition, the primary synergy for the sales reps that drive renewals and upsells is with the customer success team because of their intimacy with the requisite details to empower that conversation with the customer.

Even if this sales function does not land in the customer success organization (absorption), there will be significant influence on the sales process by the CSMs. In fact, a good sales rep will initiate and build the relationship with the CSMs knowing the value they will provide in the process. In many ways, the installed base sales rep will see the CSMs in the same way a new business sales rep sees and utilizes his sales consultant—as necessary to help close deals.

The movement of this part of sales toward customer success is inevitable because of where the synergy lies. The team driving renewals and upsells from your customer base will be joined at the hip with your customer success team. At best, there's a diminishing argument for having that team live in another organization.

Marketing

This is not a case for the CMO to report into the VP of customer success. There's no galaxy where that would make sense. But there is typically a part of marketing that starts with the word *customer*, and it's reasonable to consider whether it would make sense for that function to also live with the team that is responsible for the rest of the customer journey. Let's first examine the typical responsibilities of a customer marketing team and how they are potentially involved with, or influenced by, customer success:

- **E-mail marketing/nurturing**: the content, timing, and even voice of these messages must be heavily influenced by customer success to ensure every touch is as relevant as possible
- **Reference management**: all the information necessary to match a given prospect with the right customer reference will reside in the customer success management including industry, size, use cases, health score, reference frequency, and last reference completed
- **Community**: content and direct interaction will often be part of a CSM's responsibility
- **Webinars**: content and personal involvement will be required from the customer success team with regard to both product and domain expertise
- **User groups**: who to invite, personal involvement, and encouraging customers to attend will be the customer success team's responsibility
- **Customer summit**: agenda, content, proposed speakers, and personal involvement will all be provided or influenced by customer success

Just as with installed base sales, there's a case to be made that most of the synergy for the customer marketing team is with customer success, not with other parts of marketing. And just as with installed base sales, a CCO who owns the company retention number will have the right to ask for ownership of the tools and talent needed to deliver that number. No chief revenue officer would take that role if it didn't include the demand generation part of marketing. If you are being held responsible for the new business quota for the company, you will ask for control of the entire revenue pipeline, not just the bottom half of it. The same philosophy can be applied to customer success and the CCO. If you ask your CCO to be responsible for the entire customer journey and the sales results expected to come from the customer base, then owning all of the customer touch points, including the ones listed previously that are typically part of customer marketing, is a legitimate ask. And keep in mind the changing landscape regarding where the dollars flow from in a maturing subscription or pay-as-you-go business. See Figure 15.3 for a reminder of the reality that, over a fairly short period of time, the percentage of bookings that come from existing customers exceeds that of new business and then accelerates rapidly to the point where it could easily be six times to eight times new business. With that level of responsibility comes significant authority and organizational power.

Customer marketing may not move into customer success as rapidly as the renewals and upsell sales function, but it's being drawn in that direction already and influence is increasing daily, which might leave absorption not far behind.

Sales Consulting

This one is the road less traveled of the three and wouldn't have even made this list six weeks ago. But more progressive, and aggressive, CEOs are moving this function, which has always and forever been part of sales, into customer success. The reason is simple and logical. See Chapter 5, Customer Success Law 1, "Sell to the Right Customer."

There are a number of ways to ensure that a company enforces this law as we've discussed. Incent the sales VP on retention, give the customer success VP veto power over the pipeline, and a few others. We did not mention this one, which is to give ownership of a vital part of the sales organization to the person who has to live with the sales decisions. This is a bold statement and sure to be fought fiercely by most VPs of sales, but it's easy to see the logic in it. It's akin to taking the quality assurance function away from the VP of engineering and putting it under customer support. Assuming the leadership is competent and the necessary lines of communication with engineering don't get broken, it could be a brilliant move. Ownership of the function that blesses new product releases lies with the organization that will suffer the most pain if a bad release goes out. Not stupid. Not stupid at all.

Regardless of the organizational logic, the message this sends from the CEO is pretty hard to miss. "We will prioritize long-term retention and customer success above merely making our quarterly sales targets." Very powerful.

Figure 15.4   The Future Chief Customer Officer Organization?

The resulting organization in this brave new world, assuming all three of the above groups are added in, ends up looking like this (Figure 15.4), and no one would argue that the leader of an organization this broad and with the degree of business impact it would have, would have a Chief in charge of it.

We originally made the case for the rise of the CCO based just on the traditional post-sales functions in the enterprise. But now we've added the possibility, perhaps even the rationale, that renewal and upsell sales, customer marketing, and even sales consulting would make sense under the same umbrella. Just as SaaS and subscriptions have shifted all the power from the vendor to the customer, the same shifting sands are moving the organizational power in the enterprise from new customer acquisition to customer success. And it's probably never moving back. Technology has enabled it, and prospects and customers are being spoiled by it. And, by the way, isn't this the way the world should work? Shouldn't customers have more control than the vendors? It certainly works that way in retail and in most consumer-oriented businesses.

Like it or not, the customer is king once again or at least climbing the steps to the throne. And that makes the person responsible for the health and happiness of the king, the CCO, vital to the vendor. Not every company has a CCO today, and many won't ever have one, but the momentum of the customer success movement is accelerating the rise of this role.

16 | Customer Success Technology

When a new discipline becomes commonplace and the practitioners come together to create departments, teams, and organizations, technology is sure to follow. This is most definitely the case with customer success. As more and more people take on CSM titles or similar responsibilities, the processes and best practices around how to execute the daily tactical duties begin to coalesce. Once that starts to happen, there's room for technology to come in with the promise of improving the processes and the productivity of the people.

Customer success, whether done in a high-touch way or a tech-touch way, is all about data. Actually, it's really about turning data into information and then turning that information into action. But it starts with data. Lots of data.

A Plethora of Customer Information

Think about what almost every B2B company, and more B2C companies every day, know about their customers:

- Demographics—industry, geography, company size, and so forth
- How long they have been a customer

199

- What they have purchased and when
- What they paid for every product they have purchased
- Every invoice ever sent—when, what, amount, terms
- Every payment ever received—when, amount
- Every services/support call—when, reason, severity, response time, resolution time
- Every e-mail ever sent and result (open, bounced, unsubscribed, clicked-through)
- Every event/webinar attended or registered for
- Any direct-mail marketing sent
- Website visits and source of traffic
- Support portal visits and actions taken
- Every training class taken—classroom or on-demand
- Every survey sent, received, and any responses
- How your products are being used (anecdotally or electronically)

And if you are a subscription-based or pay-as-you-go company you will also know:

- Original contract value
- Current contract value
- Growth rate of contract
- Number of renewals completed or opt-outs not exercised

And if you are a SaaS company, this, too:

- Every action ever taken in your product (pages viewed, clicks, reports run, etc.)

Over time, this becomes an amazingly rich set of data. And data fits into the world of customer success in a very logical way—the more you know about your customers, the more effective you can be in managing them. Remember Customer Success Law 4 (Chapter 8, "Relentlessly Monitor and Manage Customer Health"). That obviously cannot be done without data. A customer health score is ultimately just a predefined analysis of a discrete set of data that is then brought together into a single score.

The value that technology can bring to customer success can be encapsulated in a few key areas:

1. Optimize CSM time
2. Increase the intelligence of every customer touch
3. Drive scalability
4. Improve collaboration, communication, and visibility
5. Better team management

Let's look at each one of these in depth.

Optimize Customer Success Management Time

The first value proposition that most customer success teams are seeking is for an early-warning system. Oftentimes, it's the existence of churn that drives the need for some kind of tooling, whether internal or off-the-shelf, to provide visibility into customer health, specifically customers at-risk. In the absence of any activity-based information, the prioritization of customer interactions is often driven, in a subscription company, by two typically well-known data points: (1) renewal date and (2) ARR (or total contract value). Number 2, as a proxy for customer value, is the one that drives prioritization for companies that don't have a specific renewal, such as those with month-to-month contracts or pay-as-you-go companies. Customer value, whatever that might mean to you, is something that transcends subscriptions and is important across all types of companies. Most CEOs would have at least a general answer to the question, "Who are your most valuable customers?" That becomes the de facto prioritization if no other information exists to help with that process. In any case, anyone actively managing customers will ultimately come up with some method of prioritization in order to optimize their time. The days of just having a regular calling schedule and relying on personal relationships with all customers are in our rearview mirror. See Chapter 9, Customer Success Law 5, "You Can No Longer Build Loyalty through Personal Relationships," for more insights on this dilemma.

The problem here is an obvious one. Customer value alone, or even value plus renewal date, is not sophisticated enough as a prioritization tool, to identify and differentiate those customers who urgently need attention, from those that are doing fine and may not need any of your time. There's a crying need for more information. This is where the quest often branches in one of two directions: (1) attempt to get product usage data or (2) get other data about other customer interactions.

- **Product usage data**: Everyone agrees that, if you could only tap into one source of data, this would be it. The best indicator of customer health and predictor of future buying behavior definitely lies with how each customer uses your product. But it can be challenging to get and even harder to trend.
- **Other customer interactions**: Customers call support, pay (or don't pay) invoices, respond (or not) to surveys, engage with your marketing messages, and so forth. These are almost always in a variety of systems that are separate and distinct. The perfect account manager would have to log into, and decipher data from, multiple other systems in order to prioritize their outreaches and maximize the value of each.

Ideally, you want all of this information, but it's often a step-by-step journey so you need to choose one battle at a time.

So, we've established that there's a need for more information in order to drive the right interactions at the right time with our customers. In addition to pure information, for which Excel or your CRM system, might suffice, there's a need for some system-driven analytics to help give context to a particular data point or set of data, and even to recommend action. This is where a customer success management solution can deliver very high value and quick wins.

Just a quick aside here. We're not doing an evaluation of any specific technology solutions nor are we even describing the specifics about what any one of them in particular can do. We're simply identifying the problems that customer success teams are experiencing and how technology can help solve those problems, whether that's an internally built solution or a third-party software purchase. And, because customer success is still in its infancy and CSM solutions came along only after the discipline of customer success came into being, the volume and sophistication of changes is very hard to predict. Suffice it to say this, the application solutions for customer success will rapidly get more robust and significantly better over the next few years.

Back to optimizing your team's time. We've laid out a pretty clear picture that is the current state for most companies—a lack of information and insights that will help with the prioritization and execution of resources against customer needs. Much of the data exists somewhere in the enterprise and more might exist externally. Bringing that data together into one place, giving one consistent view of the customer, with insights into the meaning of the information, and the recommended actions, will give any customer-centric company a huge leap forward. The old world often sounded like this:

We've got three customers coming up for renewal, or anniversary, in the next 90 days. We should definitely be talking to all three consistently starting today, especially Acme because they are our largest customer overall. Let's make sure none of them are going anywhere.

The new world will sound more like one of these:

We have 17 customers whose usage of our key features is down by more than 20 percent over the past six months and who either did not respond or gave us a negative score on our last survey. Let's contact every one of them, starting with the four that are up for renewal this quarter or are still in their first year with us. Let's also prioritize Acme because they have a 50 percent contract step-up scheduled for nine months from now.

This week's priorities are the seven customers who have P1 or P2 support cases that have been open more than 10 days and who are more than 30 days past due on their most recent invoice.

We have five customers where our executive sponsor moved on to another job or where our user champion unsubscribed after our last marketing e-mail. Let's talk to them as soon as possible.

We have over 30,000 customers who have not even tried the new collaboration feature in our last release. Let's get an e-mail out to them inviting them to view the on-demand training video and come to next week's webinar on this topic.

Consolidated, actionable information brought together into a system that triggers and tracks every customer touch, whether human or tech. That's how you prioritize customer interactions and optimize your team's time.

Increase the Intelligence of Every Customer Touch

Although this is a value proposition distinct from the first, the solution is the same one—easily accessible, high-quality information. In the absence of the right set of information, most customer interactions take the form of a check-in call.

> Hey John, it's Dan, your account manager. It's the third Thursday of the month so I'm just calling to see how things are going, and if there's anything I can do to help.

Today, our customers have every right to bristle if we make a call like that. We should know how things are going, even to the extent of knowing if/how they are using our product. Shouldn't we? Even if we don't have that elusive usage data, we still have enough to make our call much more valuable than that one. Shouldn't it sound more like this? No usage data required for this call by the way:

> Hey John, it's Dan, your account manager. I just wanted to thank you for attending our webinar last week and personally follow up to see if you needed any more information or guidance on that topic. I also noticed that you've opened up three support tickets in the past two weeks regarding reporting. Let me know if you want me to review any of the reports you are working on.

It's easy to see the value of this kind of call. It's also fairly easy to understand the pain of digging all of that information up if you don't have it consolidated somewhere. What's much harder to quantify is the cost of not digging it up. Frankly, most CSMs or account managers are so busy that they just don't have time to go log in to three or four other systems and try to find the information that would help make their next call better. So they just don't do it. The result is a whole lot of check-in calls. Not because your folks don't want to do the best job they can, but because they have to prioritize how they spend their time, and, usually, the actual customer touch is higher on the priority list than the quality of that touch. Clearly, in order to make your team more productive and intelligent, whether high touch, low touch, or tech touch, you need to bring some vital set of customer-health-related information together in one easily consumable place.

The value of this solution also goes far beyond your customer success efforts. This one delivers for every single person in your company who talks to customers. Wouldn't every one of your customer conversations be better if it was more information driven? Think about a few examples:

- **Customer support**: Your support reps talk to customers all the time. The primary source of intelligence for them is their solution (Zendesk, ServiceCloud, Parature, etc.). They can easily access how many tickets are open, how many have been closed in the past 30 days, priority and severity of each, average time-to-close, and so on. That's good, but wouldn't they benefit from also knowing current and trended health scores, open actions (not cases), last survey results, positive/negative usage trends, and invoices overdue? Customer touches are rare and precious things. Everyone in your company needs to optimize them.

- **Product Managers**: They don't talk to customers as often, but wouldn't they want to know how the customer is using their product (if it's available) and how that compares to overall use of the product across the installed base? Also, what do they own, when did they purchase it, and more.

- **Professional services**: Your consultants are interacting on engagements all the time with customers and will benefit greatly from a more well-rounded understanding of each of those customers.

- **Sales**: Whether it's an enterprise representative managing her customers forever, or a renewal or upsell rep digging in on an open opportunity, the need for deep understanding of customer health is paramount. Maybe bigger is the need to never get blind-sided when they call a customer. There's nothing worse than having a sales call derailed by a high-priority support ticket that you didn't know about.

- **Marketing**: Who usually manages the reference program, the case study program, and the user groups? Marketing. They need to be well informed about customer health and activity in order to perform any of those responsibilities well. This is one of the reasons that the customer marketing part of marketing is getting cozier and cozier with customer success as we elaborated in the previous chapter.

- **Executives**: Nobody likes to get blind-sided less than your CEO. And no employee wants to be the reason his CEO got blindsided. One of the best ways to understand the value of this proposition—all the right information consolidated in one place—is to observe the scramble that takes place to prepare a CEO for a customer call. There's probably enough effort in just a couple of those situations to justify the purchase or building of a solution.

This solution is often referred to as the *360 degree view of a customer*, and CSM technology actually makes that dream a reality for the first time. CRM systems used to claim that same phrase, but it has turned out to be far from true unless there's enormous effort expended to push information into the

CRM solution that doesn't really have another proper home. The value of solving this problem is massive and far-reaching, and the opportunity cost of not solving it is also huge but, more dangerously, it's hidden.

Drive Scalability

If there's a word in the business lexicon more often used than *scalability*, I can't imagine what it is. And when someone is talking about scalability, technology almost always has to be part of the answer. This is certainly true for customer success in which there are really only two ways to manage an ever-increasing customer base:

1. More people
2. Technology

Of course, the right answer is actually number 3—a combination of 1 and 2. Customer success, for most B2B companies, is, at least in part, a people-driven effort, and that will likely always be true. And people are always the most expensive part of any business operation. In order to improve profitability, you can't scale people linearly with customer growth, at least not for those organizations who aren't charging separately for their efforts. Not charging is usually the case for standard customer support and customer success. Both are necessary for high rates of retention and customer satisfaction, so the baseline delivery of each is typically bundled with the SaaS contract or provided to every customer in a traditional business or the on-premise software community.

Given that reality, technology must be applied to the discipline in order to improve productivity and profitability. Customer success solutions should enable a 25 percent to 30 percent improvement in productivity at a minimum. That is usually measured by the number of accounts managed per person or by the number of dollars managed per person. If I'm a high-touch CSM and have access to a great CSM solution, I should be able to increase the number of customers I can manage with the same quality, from 25 to 30 or maybe even 35. If I'm a tech-touch CSM managing 1,000 customers, the right technology could literally double that number or much more. If it's all about tech, the number of customers almost doesn't matter. Do you think Verizon worries about their customer e-mail campaigns not scaling when they add a million customers a month? Of course not. They just send more e-mails.

The aspects of a technology solution that allow for the productivity increase are pretty obvious, and we've talked about several of them already:

- Prioritization—not touching customers who don't need to be touched, which is a huge plus
- Effectiveness—information-driven insights make each call more effective
- Collaboration—we'll talk more about this shortly but making the sharing of information easier is a big plus
- Accessibility—key information is no longer hidden in e-mail but available to all
- Proactivity—the amount of effort required to be proactive is exponentially smaller than firefighting

Perhaps nothing is more important to business viability than scalability. It's why so much money is spent on technology. There are usually manual ways of doing almost everything, but technology brings efficiency, accuracy, and scalability to virtually every part of a business to which it is intelligently applied.

Improve Collaboration, Communication, and Visibility

As your customer base grows, so, too, does the size of the teams managing them. Even if you scale efficiently, you still have to scale adequately with people. More customers, more people touching customers, more layers of management, more separation of departments/responsibilities, more challenges. There's simply no way around it. When scale happens, the need to be better at collaboration and communication can equal, perhaps even exceed, the need to become more productive. That's another perfect application of technology. Systems, by definition, can bring things together. Those "things" can be the people who are doing similar jobs, the information needed to do those jobs, the status of each task, and the relevant management insights and results. All things that should be legitimately systematized.

Workflow might be an overused word, a bit like scalability. But it's used often for good reason. It's important. In the early days of customer success technology, there was an almost exclusive focus on analytics. It was all about, and only about, the data. Vendors had the word *analytics* in their company names (later changed) because they felt it was the end game. But the market always has the last say, not the vendors. And the market originally bought into the idea that it was all about analytics. The only thing better than talking about analytics was talking about predictive analytics. But that turned out to be a bit of a red herring. It's true that analytics were important and still are. It's also true that predictive analytics is a legitimate pursuit and will provide tremendous value to customer success efforts over time. But it should have never been the focal point of a company or a product, and that also applies to those creating their own solutions internally. The core problem that needs solving in customer success is not an analytics problem. If that were true, it would have been solved long ago. There's no shortage of amazing analytics solutions, from Business Objects to Birst to Good Data to Tableau. Wonderful products, all of them. And there's a place for every one of them in virtually every company but not instead of role-specific solutions alongside them. The core problem that needs to be solved, just as it is with CRM, is a collaboration and communication problem, which is solved by developing a workflow solution that addresses the daily lives of customer success people.

I mentioned CRM because it's such a great analogy for this value proposition. I'm going to expand on it a bit because everyone understands how sales works so it always makes for a good comparative. I'll use Salesforce as a proxy here for all CRM systems because I'm most familiar with it. Is Salesforce an analytics tool? For those who don't know the answer, it's "no." Or, maybe more accurately, "NO!" Is there an analytics component to Salesforce? Absolutely. Is it being refined and advanced as we speak? Absolutely. Does anyone buy Salesforce purely to do analytics? No way. There are lots of different ways of deriving value from Salesforce, especially now that it's become an amazing platform upon which thousands of other applications have been built. But the original value proposition was what was once called SFA, or sales force automation. Automating the Sales function. Salesforce, and all CRMs, create a way for Sales teams to manage and track all aspects of their world, which is all about closing deals. In Salesforce, that comes down to four buckets (objects): (1) leads, (2) contacts, (3) accounts, and

(4) opportunities. In other words, everything needed to understand and manage the sales funnel. Sales is ultimately about managing opportunities to get deals closed. This has been done since the dawn of time without a CRM system. The CRM system simply puts some structure and discipline around that process. This creates four massively valuable results for the company:

1. Predictability
2. Forecastability
3. Repeatability
4. Visibility

The results don't come without some level of pain. Ask a sales rep whose company religiously uses a CRM system. They probably spend more time than they'd like putting data into the system and then managing all of their processes there, too. But it's a necessary part of the process for the greater good of the company. Plus, if they don't do it, their VP might threaten to not pay their commissions.

These same four characteristics are needed in customer success. The only difference is that it's about existing customers, not prospects. How do these apply in the post-sales world?

- **Predictability**: A system that has all the data and tracks the workflow of the tasks associated with CSM role creates the ability for future results to become predictable.
- **Forecastability**: As with sales, customer success must forecast renewals, upsell, and churn. Only a system using the right information and applying historical results appropriately can help codify and refine accurate forecasts.
- **Repeatability**: Only if the workflow of the individuals is tracked (think pipeline management) can a system then be used to determine what worked and what didn't so you can repeat what worked and throw away what didn't.
- **Visibility**: CRM systems are especially good at providing management visibility into individual deals or company-wide pipeline and forecasts. A great CSM solution will provide the same insights for customers.

I mention visibility, which is the third of the pillars of this value proposition. The other two are collaboration and communication, which we danced around and touched on but didn't address explicitly. Simply put, collaboration and communication go hand-in-hand with workflow. A complete workflow engine will include a communication function that allows for the free flow of information and commentary designed to keep all parties in sync. An example of this is Salesforce's Chatter product, which enables in-product communication so that it can be captured in context and does not get buried in an individual's e-mail. CSM systems will typically take advantage of existing technology such as Chatter or Yammer but could certainly build their own, too. Proper, in-product communication is the way to keep your CEO from asking, "What's the latest on Acme?" when he's thinking about them. The aforementioned 360-degree view of the customer addresses some of that question, but specific commentary from those who have recently touched that customer will put the period at the end of the sentence. In-product communication can be done, and often is, through comment fields, but most would agree that has too many shortcomings to be a great long-term solution.

Collaboration, though similar, is distinct from communication. Collaboration is not just commentary but also a way to share, to distribute, and to cooperate on specific tasks and activities. In a CRM system, that might include a way to create and store a quote or a proposal that your boss can then edit and refine. A CSM system will need that same capability, perhaps even more so because of the need to delegate tasks and actions to others. Customer success, by its nature, will involve people outside the team in order to solve customer challenges. Sales is more self-contained. Although your CEO and other execs may get involved in specific sales deals, specific tasks are not as often delegated to someone outside of sales. It's not that this never happens; it's just less common than in customer success. CSMs are constantly in need of assistance to drive success for their customers. That could mean involving a product manager to talk about the intricacies of how a part of the product works or to talk about a future feature. It might mean involving a support rep to troubleshoot a particular issue. It could mean delegating an executive outreach up to their VP or CEO. And, of course, it will often involve temporary involvement on the part of engineering. In any case, the CSM solution must allow for the necessary sharing, delegating, and general collaboration around any given task or activity.

As teams and companies grow, collaboration and communication become more and more important. It's not so much that they surpass productivity in importance, it's that they become necessary *in order to* improve productivity.

Better Team Management

It's true that the primary purpose of CSM technology is to help teams manage their customers more effectively. However, it's equally true that if the solution is robust and includes workflow as described in the previous section, you'll have a system with the potential to be just as effective at helping you manage your team.

Let's again look at a CRM system as an example. CRM systems, at least when they were exclusively SFA, were designed to help manage the sales process. They provide structure and enforce discipline with regard to keeping deals in the pipeline and moving them through the pipeline. The VP of sales relies on the CRM system to tell him when to squeeze marketing for more leads (as if there's ever a day when that doesn't happen), let the CEO know where the risks are, and generally manage to his forecast. This is why CRM is so sticky; it's ultimately invaluable to both the CEO and the CFO.

Although that was the original design and intent, an ancillary value was quickly discovered. The CRM system helped manage the team. It's almost unfair to use the word *helped* in that sentence. The CRM system has become the primary management tool for the VP of sales. All of the activities and results that can tell the VP if an individual sales rep is on the right track, aside from just closing deals, will be found in the CRM system:

- Calls made
- Meetings completed
- Pipeline growth
- Proposals created
- Pipeline movement
- Stuck deals
- Deals/dollars closed
- Days-to-close
- Average selling price (ASP)

That information is gold if you're running a sales team. Each one of those data points tells you something really important. And, then, even more valuable is comparing those data points across all members of the team. That allows you to benchmark, to create competition, and to focus your coaching. It also allows the VP to take advantage of the specific areas of expertise of each individual rep and use their skills to upgrade everyone else on the team. Every team is made up of various strengths and weaknesses. The job of the leader is to maximize the strengths and minimize the weaknesses. His CRM system is his best friend in this process, and it will be a rare one-on-one in which it's not at the forefront of the discussion.

I know I'm belaboring the analogy between CRM and CSM, but it's so clear that a great CSM solution will accomplish many of the same successes in much the same way as a CRM system. It all revolves around the central value proposition derived from workflow. Giving a CSM a system that becomes their workspace, their to-do list, their activity tracker, their prioritization engine, and their communication and collaboration vehicle also means that everything needed to measure their effectiveness and coach them up is in that same system. The ability to track the important activities is the same as with a CRM—the activities themselves are the only variable:

- Calls made
- Meetings completed
- Actions triggered
- Actions closed (by category)
- QBRs completed
- Other milestones completed
- Renewals/upsell results
- Customer health score
- Customer satisfaction score
- E-mails sent/opened/clicked-on
- Account plans created/updated

For most of customer success's short history, CSM one-on-ones have been pretty fluffy. Questions such as "Are all your customers happy?" "Any customers at risk?" "How can I help?" were predominant. But a great CSM solution changes all that and makes life significantly better for both the individual CSM and the VP. After all, great employees want clear and measurable targets for which they are held accountable and for which they are rewarded when they meet and exceed them. And great leaders want the same for themselves and for their teams so they can justify and reward the proper behavior. And, like the sales VP, they want to identify the strengths and weaknesses across their team that they can then manage accordingly. There's much more on customer success becoming metrics focused in Chapter 13, Customer Success Law 9, "Drive Customer Success through Hard Metrics."

Another aspect of managing a team effectively is to clearly understand the capacity of the team and to staff for maximum effectiveness within the expense constraints of the company. The CSM solution will be an invaluable part of that process. As we've mentioned previously, customer success is a revenue-driving organization just like sales. That means that the justification for additional headcount comes from revenue or bookings. "Everyone on the team is really busy" will no longer work with your CEO. You'll need to clearly articulate the bottom line value derived from each additional CSM, and only the insights provided by a CSM solution that is helping you track all of the measurables that matter can assist you in that task.

Those are the key value propositions that CSM technology can bring to a team, but that list is far from exhaustive. We didn't mention reporting, dashboards, surveys, data integration, visualization, e-mail functionality, cohort analysis, account planning, CRM integration, external data tracking, and many other functions that are necessary parts of a full-function solution. And remember, this journey is only three to four years along. What's available today is truly just the tip of the iceberg.

There's one last benefit that comes from a great customer success technology solution. Because customer success is such a young organization, one struggle has been to truly have a seat at the executive table. Most of those seats exist because of the traditional value they've provided over the years. They belong to VPs of sales, CMOs, CFOs, CTOs, VPs of engineering, COOs, VPs of operations, CIOs, and so forth. As we discussed at length in the previous chapter, the power shift happening at many companies and the rise of the CCO is changing this. But technology that enables the customer success leader to quantify his value and present objective results to that end is a valuable participant in that endeavor. It's not a new idea. Virtually every other major organization has a domain-specific application, which helps them manage their business and their teams, quantify their results, and justify their additional needs. Customer success is simply the latest entry into that game. The bottom line is that major organizations require empowered leaders, and empowered leaders need technology assistance. That's happening rapidly in the new world of customer success.

17 | Where Do We Go from Here?

This is where we talk about flying cars, right? Doesn't every story that looks to the future have flying cars in it? In this case, perhaps those flying cars are actually Google self-flying cars. And, of course, they will be carrying customer success droids that, at a cost of a penny apiece, will come on-site with every single customer of our products and guide them through the perfect use and the highest possible ROI. Churn will be a distant memory. Every customer will be a customer for life. The next generation always has it *so* much easier.

Okay. Time to awaken from that dream and spend some additional time here in the real world. No doubt the future will bring dramatic changes to every part of our lives. Customer success will not be left behind. In fact, because it's still in its infancy and because of its dependency on technology, the pace of change is likely to be significantly higher than in most disciplines.

Predicting the future and what will and won't change is a dangerous business, although it's always a no-brainer to simply say "everything will change." I know for sure that many of the elements of customer success we've discussed in this book will continue to morph and mature and many others will take their place in the spotlight at various times. If this book is not completely out of date in a couple years, I'll be surprised and disappointed. Greater things lie ahead. Here are a number of areas of change, or further change, that are likely:

1. Customer success will continue to grow in importance beyond SaaS.
2. CCO as a role/title will continue to emerge.
3. The discipline of customer success will become more defined and refined.
4. Customer success as an organization will become more operationally focused and less relationship dependent.
5. Businesses will recognize and quantify the value of customer success.
6. Demand for customer success experience will continue to outstrip supply.
7. Universities will start to teach customer success.
8. Technology improvement will accelerate rapidly and customer success solutions will become must-have instead of nice-to-have.
9. CEOs who came up through customer success will become commonplace.
10. Customer success operations will become as logical and necessary as sales operations.
11. "One-to-many CSM" will appear as a job description and be a highly valued position.
12. Birds-of-a-feather gatherings around customer success will become less interesting because there will be so many people in customer success that we'll all know others in the role.
13. Big players, in addition to more start-ups, will enter the technology market.
14. Some current technology provider will create a dominant position and do an IPO.
15. The sighting of VPs of customer success on the podium for the IPO bell-ringing will be frequent.
16. Earnings calls will consistently focus on retention and call out customer success.
17. The phrase *customer success* will appear on the cover of *Information Week* or *Forbes* or *Fortune* or some such publication.
18. Overall churn rates will not decline because the friction to switch vendors will continue to decrease as fast as the practice of customer success improves.
19. Major management consulting firms will build practices around customer success.
20. Numerous books will be written on the topic.

The Customer Economy

As SaaS companies mature and virtually every company tries to become a recurring revenue business, it's easy to predict that the value and visibility of customer success will continue to rise. In those recurring revenue businesses, customer success is an imperative and, as such, will always have its place in the spotlight. But other businesses, driven by the power shift from the vendor to the customer, will be also required to embrace some of the philosophy and practices of customer success. Remember that customer success is a secondary wave, not the primary one. The primary wave is the move to recurring revenue business models, which places customers on the throne. At the same time, customers (businesses and consumers) continue to gain power in the market dynamic because of social media and the easy availability of all information. No vendor can hide from its failures, and its success stories will spread quickly, with or without a public relations team. It is, without question, the Age of the Customer. In fact, I'll take Tien Tzuo's phrase "the subscription economy" one step further and coin a new and broader term—*the customer economy*.

In the customer economy, the customer (surprise!) will have more and more power. We've seen this happen over the course of the Internet age as information becomes more easily accessible than ever. This trend has almost certainly not run its course. Tsunamis grow in height as they approach the shore, which is why they are so destructive. The subscription tsunami is still building and is a long way from the shore and its maximum height and disruptive power. We've seen the tip of the iceberg in the software world, but this tsunami will not be limited to the disruption of one market. The software industry has been massively disrupted by subscriptions and the web as a delivery vehicle. Given that, it's easy and logical to extrapolate disruption across virtually every other industry, too. One needs to look no further than the taxi business, disrupted by Uber and Lyft, and the hotel business, disrupted by Airbnb, to see this happening before our eyes. Every one of those disruptions is beneficial to the customer because they provide options. Better options. Nothing will stop that. If customers see a better way, they will have it. Cities and unions can fight Uber all they want. In the end, they can't win. The customer, en masse, will always win.

So if every business is going to get disrupted in favor of the customer, then every business is going to have to turn more focus and energy and investment on caring for their customers. That's the nature of customer success. What's been done so far is amazing, but there really are miles to go before we sleep. Those who adapt the quickest will survive and those who embrace the customer movement will take advantage of it as opposed to being stampeded by it. Those are pretty much the only two choices. You can choose to be Waldenbooks and fight Amazon and the Internet (and lose) or you can be Barnes & Noble and embrace the Internet, compete with Amazon at their own game, and survive. The customer is becoming more important, and more empowered, in every business in the world, including yours. It's time to start thinking seriously about customer success.

Ideal Customer Success Today

Rather than dreaming about flying cars and customer success droids, it will be more practical and probably more helpful to just talk about what an ideal customer experience could be today, especially with so many companies just getting started on this journey. In essence, the perfect execution of customer success today will feel very futuristic to most. Let's dig in and see what that might look like.

Fictional vendor: Wingtip Software, Inc Wingtip is a SaaS company delivering an online training solution to SMB and midmarket customers. They've been in business for five years with solid growth that has them poised to finish 2015 with $40 million in ARR across 1,600 customers. Overall ASP is now at $25,000 but rising. It was $21,000 when the year started and will exceed $35,000 in the fourth quarter. Wingtip has stopped selling below $10,000 annual contracts but still have about 200 of those customers on the books. At the high end, they've begun pushing into Enterprise customers and have 15 whose ARR is over $150,000. At their investors' insistence, they invested early on in customer success, knowing their business depended on it. Their VP of customer success was employee number 23 (out of now 320 total employees). He has responsibility for all post-sales functions, which includes onboarding, training, customer support, professional services, and classic customer success. His total team is 110 people 21, of whom are on the classic customer success team. They break down into these functions:

- Thirteen are midmarket CSMs with two of them focused on the top 25 customers, while the other 11 manage about 50 each.

- Four are SMB CSMs who manage 600 customers in a pooled model.
- One CSM has responsibility for creating the one-to-many programs used by all the CSMs and manages the remaining customers in a pure tech-touch model.
- Two are directors, one over midmarket and one over SMB/tech touch.
- One is a customer success operations person, soon to be two.

Fictional customer: Financiality, Inc. Financiality is a technology and services company providing data analytics tools and consulting to banks and brokers. It purchased the Wingtip solution because it needed a tool to help the company easily create and track on-demand product training. Financiality made its purchase at the end of Wingtip's 2014 second quarter (Q2) and signed a one-year deal for $29,000 ARR plus a onetime $15,000 for the Mid-Market onboarding package.

Financiality falls into Wingtip's low-touch customer segment. That means that the planned experience is a combination of one-on-one touches and automated touches. Reality is not often exactly what is planned so the actual experience has been something like this so far:

- June 30, 2014—Financiality signs the contract with Wingtip.
- July 1, 2014—the necessary details from the Wingtip CRM system get automatically pushed to the customer success system and the appropriate project manager and CSM are automatically assigned to the account based on an algorithm that takes into account both workload and a round-robin system.
- July 1, 2014—Financiality's senior director of education, Joe Smith, who signed the contract, receives a personalized e-mail from the Wingtip CEO, automatically triggered from their CRM system, welcoming him to the Wingtip family. The letter also introduces Wingtip's onboarding project manager, Shannon Jones, and outlines the expected next steps.
- July 1, 2014—Shannon contacts Joe via e-mail to set up the project kickoff call.
- July 2, 2014—Joe receives through Amazon a thank-you gift from Wingtip that was automatically triggered by the closing of the contract. Based on the sales rep's choice selected in their CRM system, it's a high-quality key chain bearing Wingtip's logo and Joe's name.
- July 2, 2014—Shannon studies the information about Financiality in the Wingtip CRM system to determine whether she has any questions for the sales team before proceeding with the project. It appears to be

right in their sweet spot so she chooses to proceed without initiating a handoff meeting.

- July 2, 2014—Shannon receives an out-of-office response to her e-mail from Joe saying that Joe will be on PTO until July 14.
- July 2, 2014—Shannon immediately flags the onboarding project as at risk because her SLA for project completion is eight weeks from contract signature and a two-week delay on the start date makes that SLA highly unlikely.
- July 15, 2014—Joe responds to Shannon's request for a kickoff meeting, and they schedule it for July 16.
- July 16, 2014—Shannon and Joe and two of Joe's key team members hold the kickoff meeting and review the project plan. A few tweaks are made, but the key milestones are agreed upon, including the go-live date of September 5.
- July 16, 2014—Shannon updates the Wingtip customer success system with the key milestone dates and leaves the project in the *at-risk* state because the projected Go-Live date is past her eight-week SLA.
- August 14, 2014—The third milestone of five is successfully completed on schedule. An automated e-mail is triggered from the customer success system to Joe and his project team, introducing them to their CSM, Mary Harrison, and informing them that she will be inserting herself into key meetings over the next few weeks as they near go-live.
- August 15, 2014—Mary begins to monitor Financiality's product usage in the customer success system and sets up a standard set of rules that, if triggered, will notify her via e-mail. Some of the rules are risk based (25 percent drop-off in usage) and some are opportunities (more than 80 percent of Financiality's licenses are active). She also triggers the creation of an Account Health Score in the customer success system, which will start tracking overall customer health for Financiality taking into account their purchase date and planned use cases.
- September 5, 2014—All items on the project plan are complete and the go-live meeting happens. Shannon and Mary jointly lead the meeting as they transition Financiality from one to the other. Financiality signs off on the completion of the project and Mary officially takes over account responsibility from Shannon.
- September 8, 2014—Joe receives an onboarding assessment survey that was automatically sent to him from the Wingtip customer success system based on the completion of the Go-Live milestone. Joe responds and gives the project a satisfaction score of 5 out of 5.
- September 8, 2014—Because the project satisfaction score was 4 or higher, the *at-risk* tag on Financiality is removed in the customer success

system, which raises their overall health score to 78 which is at the very high end of the Q2 cohort.

- September 30, 2014—90 days after contract signature, Joe and all of the Wingtip users at Financiality receive their first NPS survey from Wingtip, automatically triggered from their customer success solution.
- October 7, 2014—Mary receives a notification from her customer success system that one user responded to the survey with a detractor score of 4. Mary immediately follows up directly with the user and helps her get back on track.
- September 11–November 3—Three different notifications occur in the Wingtip customer success system that new users at Financiality have logged into the Wingtip system but viewed fewer than three pages in the following seven days. This triggers an automated e-mail to each of the users with some tips and tricks and a pointer to the on-demand "Getting Started with Wingtip" video training. The response of all three users is tracked in the customer success system as they each open the e-mail and click on the video after which their usage increases noticeably in the following week.
- September 23 and following—Every user, when they've reached the thresholds of both 50 logins and 500 pageviews, receives an electronic $10 Starbucks card in their e-mail, automatically triggered from Wingtip's customer success system.
- November 17, 2014—Mary receives a notification that Financiality has opened five support cases in the past seven days. This is a danger signal, and she follows up with Joe and schedules a review with her director of support to ensure closure on all issues.
- December 8, 2014—Mary conducts a video executive business review (EBR) to review progress over the first 90 days and plan milestones for the next 90. This first EBR is done live, but she explains to Financiality that future EBRs will consist of PowerPoint slides following the same format automatically sent to them from her customer success solution along with an automated survey regarding goals for the next 90 days.

I realize that was a little bit tedious, but the first 90 days of a customer's life is so important, and it's essential to understand the kind of experience you can create for your customers with the right tools and processes. Remember also that the biggest risk of churn is at the time of first renewal or early on in the customer's life cycle if there isn't a renewal event. Managing the customer experience really well from day one is critical.

Without going into all the details we did above, some of the additional activities that are likely or certain to also take place in the first year with this customer will include:

- Automated surveys sent after every closed support case.
- Automated EBR PowerPoints sent every 90 days.
- Another NPS survey sent 90 days before renewal.
- Automated notification of coming renewal along with the renewal quote.
- Automated e-mails due to triggers on additional risks or opportunities.
- Occasional one-on-one outreaches with Mary, or, because it's past the first 90 days, another CSM in the pool. The need for a one-on-one is determined by the nature of the risk or opportunity.
- Annual outreaches from the Wingtip executive sponsor for Financiality.
- Another gift automatically triggered when the renewal transaction takes place.

If you read through that first-year process again, you'll see that it was not perfect. The onboarding process started and ended late. There were risks that came up both for low survey score and for too many support tickets opened. But each of those was handled quickly and efficiently, which is all a customer can really expect. In addition, there were moments of delight built into the process, too. I believe that, barring anomalous circumstances, Financiality is highly likely to renew their contract for at least another year assuming Wingtip's product provides them real business value.

For many of you, the scenario I've described feels like a pipe dream, which is why I've placed it here in this chapter. It's all very doable today so, in that sense, it's not future. But I daresay that, for most companies, this scenario feels very futuristic.

Starbucks and Customer Success

Lest you still have a feeling that customer success is only for B2B SaaS companies, let me conclude with a personal story and an analysis of customer success that is not called that but has all the same characteristics.

I love Starbucks. I don't like the taste of coffee, but I love Starbucks. I know many of you don't love Starbucks and maybe even have strong negative emotions about them for whatever reason. It's my understanding that coffee experts (a.k.a. snobs) do not favor Starbucks coffee but are more likely to be found at Peet's, Philz, Caribou, Tim Hortons, or even Dunkin' Donuts. I'm not here to argue about the quality and taste of coffee. As I said, I don't even like the taste of coffee. And, by the way, caffeine does not affect me at all. However, did I mention that I love Starbucks? Let me share with you why and see whether you agree that some of these six characteristics can be categorized as customer success:

1. Their stores are ubiquitous so there's always one nearby for a meeting outside the office in any city.
2. They offer free Wi-Fi at every store so it's an office away from the office, or home, whenever you need it.
3. There's always room to sit and often really comfortable places to sit, too. There's also almost always an outdoor seating option.
4. There's never any pressure to buy something, or to buy more, no matter how long you stay.
5. The staff is almost always friendly, even seeming to go out of their way to be friendly. There are at least three stores I frequent where they know my usual order, my name, or both.
6. The same products for the same prices (except for airports) are available in every store.

That's a starter list anyway. As many of you know, familiarity is a really good thing, especially when you travel. It's fun to try new things, but familiar things remind us of home and give us trust and comfort. This is why McDonalds is so popular even in places where it seems crazy for anyone to eat at McDonald's. For me, wherever I travel, it's easy to find a Starbucks for breakfast, an afternoon pit stop, or a convenient place to meet someone.

To me, all of those things add up to customer success. They create behavioral loyalty first, because it's almost always convenient. And then, at least for me but clearly for millions of others, too, they also create attitudinal loyalty. I have used the word *love* multiple times already to describe my loyalty to Starbucks. That's the key word that defines attitudinal loyalty. And, as we've discussed, at its core, customer success is all about creating attitudinal loyalty. Attitudinal loyalty is hard to come by. As we mentioned, it's first of all expensive. But it's also just plain hard. Do you know anyone who loves her gas station? Do you know anyone who loves her pharmacy? Do you know anyone who loves her Post Office? You might be saying, "Well, that's not fair because all of those are commodities offering the same products or services." And I say, "What about coffee? Is there any food item, with the possible exception of Coke, that is more of a commodity than coffee?" How many places do you drive by every day where you could get a cup of coffee and for far less money? And yet Starbucks stores are everywhere, often with lines of people waiting to order. Is there any other brand that you can name that creates lines? No doubt the brand that comes to mind is my premier example of attitudinal loyalty—Apple. If you are Starbucks and the loyalty of your customers is compared to that of Apple customers, you will take that six days a week and twice on Sundays.

If Starbucks counted only on its customers' need or desire for coffee, would they spend the extra money to have stores with places to sit? Of course not. That's expensive. Would they spend money on thousands and thousands of green umbrellas for outdoor seating? Certainly not. That, too, is expensive. If all Starbucks stood for was serving coffee, every store would be a drive-thru. It would not have invested in customer success to drive attitudinal loyalty and be reaping the benefits of it. As I write this, Starbucks's market cap is just short of $81 billion. That's 25 percent larger than Costco's as a comparative.

Remember now, we're not talking about customer service. We're talking about customer success. Customer service would only mean ensuring the quality of your drink, that you got what you ordered, and that it was ready in a reasonable amount of time. Making room for the customers to lounge, offering free Wi-Fi, and getting to know them by name is going beyond customer service to customer success.

There's one more thing that Starbucks has done to solidify its public appeal, and its hold on me, which has extended its vision of customer success. Starbucks has created a frequent-buyer program and married it with the latest technology to create a killer combination.

The first Starbucks card was offered to the general public in November 2001. In the next eight months, over 4 million Starbucks cards were activated. As a comparison, more cards than that will likely be activated on a single day in late December of this year. In any case, the Starbucks card has also become ubiquitous. It's perhaps the most popular gift item in history. It creates loyalty on the part of the owner. And it serves as the hook for many new customers who aren't yet regular visitors. Not a new idea by any means but genius in this market.

And then it took the loyalty program one step further. Starbucks put it on my smartphone. Long before PayPal Wallet, Apple Pay, or Android Pay appeared on the landscape, Starbucks had digitized its loyalty program and allowed me to put it on my phone. They then invested in scanners in every single store so I can pay with my phone. Today, fully 20 percent of all Starbucks purchases are paid for with a mobile device. And, if that wasn't enough, Starbucks then did one more thing that some might consider insidious. It started rewarding me for every purchase. Bonus stars they call them. Every 12 purchases, and on my birthday, I get a free drink. That doesn't sound like much but it locks you in. Just like when you get a certain number of miles on United. It becomes harder and harder to book a flight on another airline. If I'm going to sit and have a cup of coffee, I might as well do it at a place that feels like home and that rewards me for shopping there. And now the promotions roll in every week—buy one of these, get three stars. Buy two for friends, get six bonus stars. And on it goes. And it works. Frequent-buyer programs always work. They wouldn't exist if they didn't, right? That's taking a consumer retail experience and extending it so that it's subscription-like. And sometime soon, I'm sure I'll be able to buy a monthly Starbucks subscription that offers me unlimited access to my habit.

Digitizing the loyalty program is just the start, too. The app also allows me to automatically reload my card when it drops below a certain balance, which removes the conscious expenditure, something every business in the world would like to do with their customers. In some ways, it's even better than a subscription—all the benefits but there's nothing unlimited about it. Every drink and every food item is paid for. Today, I can also order ahead from my app so my drink is ready when I get there, and Starbucks delivery is not far behind.

Of course, the real magic of a loyalty program is that we as consumers think we're benefiting (which we are) when the real benefits are going to the vendor. And I'm not talking about financial benefits here. I'm talking about information. We don't have to look very far to find companies that probably know more about us than we'd like them to. Facebook, Amazon, and Google and whichever company's browser I use, come quickly to mind. Think about the value of the information Starbucks has about me and millions of others. I'm certain that Starbucks could tell you the temperature outside of every store in the country based on the ratio of hot to cold drinks it serves. Starbucks could also measure the intensity of a storm in the area based on the drop in business on that day.

Taken to the extreme, this kind of information is dangerous and perhaps even illegal. I've often wondered whether United knows that I'll pay $69 for a window seat and therefore tells me that the only standard-fare seats left on the flight I'm booking are center seats, even when it's not true. I'm not sayin'; I'm just sayin'. Starbucks can most certainly predict my behavior when it sends me a promotion that requires that I buy my favorite drink. That's not hard. But it probably also knows how far out of my comfort zone I am willing to go to earn a bonus star. Would I buy something I've never tried? Or something I've only had three times? With its volume, Starbucks can experiment daily. If it wants to know, it will know.

But we're back to attitudinal loyalty. The loyalty that Starbucks has created with me has convinced me to share information that I would otherwise not share. It has also convinced me to let Starbucks market all of its promotions to me (or spam if you prefer). It has even convinced me to basically withdraw money directly from my bank account every time I buy a drink. If the art of customer success is to create attitudinal loyalty, then Starbucks has reaped the extraordinary benefits of creating that kind of loyalty with millions of customers like me.

I acknowledged up front that not everyone loves Starbucks. But I wanted to share Starbucks' story of customer success because I think it's easier to understand than some B2B vendor selling software that you'll never use. However, that B2B vendor's customer success challenge is very much the same as Starbucks' or United Airlines'—investing in people, technology, and processes that create a customer experience that delivers attitudinal loyalty. Once a company has done that, it has paved a golden trail to overall success because attitudinal loyalty lasts. It does not go away with one bad experience. Remember that the word involved is *love*. It almost always takes a series of mistakes to change *love* to *like* or *don't mind* or *hate*. Attitudinal loyalty is money in your bank account that you can draw on as needed, knowing that you won't drain it unless you withdraw frequently. And companies that have invested in customer success and take it seriously are unlikely to ever drain their loyalty accounts dry.

Customer success, amid the customer economy, is not a cool idea or a nice thing to do. It's a necessity. Your customers expect it, or, if they don't, they soon will. And there's a growing set of expertise and technology available to help you take the first steps or to help you develop industry-leading processes for delivering the best possible customer experience. It's not rocket science, and it's not even a new idea. It's just an idea whose time has most certainly come.

Committing to customer success is hard and executing on it is expensive. But it's a necessity in many businesses already and soon will be in yours. You can resist it or embrace it. Your choice. I suggest you embrace it, and it's my sincere hope that some of the insights and practical suggestions in this book will help you along the way. I wish you the best of luck in your journey.

Index